The word Legend describes Ray Christensen. Nobody has ever been more dedicated or has done a better job as a play-by-play man for all sports in Minnesota. And nobody has the all-around ability of Ray to do news, music, or anything else.

Sid Hartman
WCCO Radio and *Star Tribune:*
Newspaper of the Twin Cities

When you think of University of Minnesota basketball, one of the first people who comes to mind is Ray Christensen. He is truly the "Voice of Golden Gopher Basketball. " We are indeed fortunate to have him as a part of our "family."

Clem Haskins
Minnesota Gophers basketball coach

Ray and I have worked together since KUOM days. Although a true intellectual, he doesn't try to overpower you with that intelligence. He's as comfortable with Mozart and Bach as he is with Giel and Kapp. And he does a terrific "Freddie the Freight Elevator."

Roger Erickson
WCCO Radio

Ray Christensen and Gopher Sports . . . the antithesis of an oxymoron. They go hand-in-hand together and have for over 40 years.

McKinley Boston
University of Minnesota
Men's Athletic Director

Golden Memories

Ray Christensen

with Stew Thornley

NODIN PRESS
Minneapolis

ISBN 0–931714–52–4

Nodin Press, a division of Micawber's, Inc.
525 North Third Street
Minneapolis, MN 55401

Second Printing

To Ramona.

This book tells of my life.

Ramona is my life.

As a play-by-play broadcaster, I try always to forget the last game and look ahead to the next one. With that kind of mental blocking out, it's often difficult to bring back memories. With the considerable help of Stew Thornley, I've tried to be as accurate as possible. Where I may fall short, I ask your forgiveness. The most important game in my broadcast career has always been the one coming up.

It still is.

R. C.

Listening to Ray Christensen in his years as a sportscaster has always been a pleasure. To team up with him—and to get to know him personally as we worked together on this book—has been a rare experience. He's seen it all and remembers it well.

S. T.

The authors would like to thank the following people for their help in obtaining photographs for this book: Wendell Vandersluis, the University of Minnesota's athletic department photographer, as well as the staff of the University's Sports Information Department; Jerry Stebbins; Paul Bergly of WCCO Radio; Bob Hagan of the Minnesota Vikings; Bob Jansen and Laura Scher of the *Star Tribune, Newspaper of the Twin Cities;* and Bonnie Wilson of the Minnesota Historical Society.

Contents

I have received many fine letters in my years of broadcasting, but the most significant one came in 1951, my first year of doing Gopher football, from a group of about 20 young men at the Faribault School for the Blind. They said that, through my descriptions, they were able to "see" the Gopher game.

Many years later, the young man who had organized that letter came up to me at the Minnesota State Fair. "You won't remember this," he told me, "but many years ago I sent you a letter from the Minnesota School for the Blind."

"I do remember," I told him and quoted a couple of lines from the letter. He was very pleased about that, and we had a good conversation. I was glad to have the chance to thank him in person and let him know how much that letter continued to mean to me.

I hope that, for all my listeners, my play-by-play helps them to understand that game, to "see" it and to "feel" it.

Ray Christensen

The Christensen family: Svend, Hilda, and Raymond.

Formative Years

I was born May 6, 1924 in Swedish Hospital in Minneapolis. It seems like a strange place for my entry into the world because I'm Dane all the way.

My father, Svend Christian Christensen, was from Denmark and my mother, Hilda Emilie Jacobsen, might as well have been. She was born in 1899 in Carlston Township, Minnesota, just north of the Iowa state line. The closest town of any size was Alden, which is a little bit west of Albert Lea.

The farmland there was rich, but the farmers were a mixture of national backgrounds. Many of the Danes decided to move to Partridge, Minnesota, about 100 miles north of the Twin Cities. My mother's family was among those making the move. Partridge was renamed Askov, and it was indeed just about 100 percent Danish. The soil, though, was far less rich than that of southern Minnesota, and, for a time, it seemed that only rutabagas could grow and survive. Askov proclaimed itself "Rutabaga Capital of the World," which it may well have been. Now, I'm told, when Askov holds its special summer celebration, the rutabagas have to be imported from Wisconsin.

Although she never traveled to Denmark in her life, my mother spoke fluent Danish. Throughout elementary school, all of her classes — with the exception of English — were taught in Danish. Later, she worked as a linotype operator for the *Askov American* under Hjalmer Petersen (later the Lieutenant Governor of Minnesota). Coming to Minneapolis when she was 20, she got a job working in the home of the Davies family, which owned Davies Mortuary.

My father was born in the village of Ørding on the island of Mors. A bridge now connects Mors to the northwestern portion of the Jutland Peninsula, but it was entirely separated from the mainland at that time. He came to the United States in 1912, docking in New York and settling in the Twin Cities, which seemed to be a magnet for people coming to this country from that part of Denmark.

He worked for a time on a dairy farm and delivered milk until he joined the U. S. Army during World War I. He was very proud of his service to this country. Every Fourth of July and Armistice Day he put on his uniform (which attests to how trim he was able to stay through the years).

He was a member of Company C of the Third Pioneer Infantry and fought in the Argonne, one of the major battle areas in France. He ended up with some shrapnel in the palm of his hand. It was a small piece, and I suppose, had he ever gone to a doctor, it could have been removed, but I think he thought of it as a badge of honor. I remember, as a child, being fascinated by that piece, that little lump in the palm of my father's hand. He and my mother, according to his wishes, are now buried at Fort Snelling Military Cemetery.

My mother was still working for the Davies family in the early 1920s when she and my father met at the Danish Young People's Home, a popular gathering spot for Danes in south Minneapolis. They were married in 1923, built a house at 4120 39th Avenue South, and the following year had their only child.

My mother wanted to name me Svend, after my father, but he wanted a more American name for me so they settled on Raymond. My middle name was Poul, after my paternal grandfather, but they later changed it to Paul, the American spelling.

Our last name has been subjected to a variety of spellings—and pronunciations—by others. Often, the name ends up being spelled with an "son" at the end, the Norwegian/Swedish version, instead of "sen", which is Danish. Of course, people sometimes say it "Chris-chen-sen" instead of its correct pronunciation, "Chris-ten-sen." You get used to it. It's no big deal.

When I was a boy, my parents watched their money carefully. My father owed no one, but we did not have a lot of money to be spent foolishly. I don't remember ever feeling that I was deprived of anything I wanted, but I do remember that we always had to respect not only the dollar, but the nickel and the penny as well. Every purchase that did not fall into the category of "necessity" was given considerable thought and, more often than not, given a "no" vote.

However, once a month, without fail, my mother bought T-bone steaks for the three of us. For supper that night, we had steak, with small round potatoes, fixed in the pan with a little butter and a little parsley. The steak and potatoes were so good and, coming just once a month, so special, that it made them "gourmet."

As a child, I spoke Danish at home although my parents made sure I was exposed to the English language as well. My English did have a Danish accent to it, and the neighborhood kids sometimes teased me about it, especially when I tried to say "three." It came out "tree." It didn't bother me, and I'm glad it didn't because I've always been grateful to my parents for enabling me to grow up with two languages.

Needless to say, my family's Danish roots remained a big

part of my life. We often went to the Danish Home, where my parents met, located only a few blocks from our house. The Danish Home is no longer there, but I remember it well. It was a big house with a great porch extending all the way around. Christmas there was always special. They had a huge Christmas tree with lighted candles (which would make fire officials cringe today). It was loaded with paper heart-shaped baskets, brimming with hard candies and cookies. The candies couldn't compare with the *pebernødder*, the pepper nut cookies, which were really hard, but well worth the challenge to eat.

We'd dance around that tree, singing *Nu har vi jul igen* ("Now we have Christmas again"), and then suddenly change directions. It was almost like a game of Crack the Whip.

I also enjoyed looking at the soccer trophies at the Danish Home. Each of the different nationalities had a soccer team at that time, and the various ethnic teams would play each other. My dad was the goaltender for the Danish team. That was the extent of his sports background though. He left his legacy in the form of trees and shrubs you can still find throughout Minneapolis.

While still a boy in Denmark, my dad had been trained and served an apprenticeship as a gardener. He went to what they called a *Planteskole* (a "plant school"), which could be compared to the vocational schools we have here, and worked in a nursery at the age of 14. Although he delivered milk when he first came to this country, he went to work as a gardener for the Minneapolis Park Board upon his discharge from the army.

For 36 years, until he retired in 1955, he tended a variety of Park Board gardens in the city. He often said, "Trees live long, but inevitably they must die. Flowers can be immortal." Even so, my father planted many of the elm trees in

14

the city and that's why it's still a little sad for me to see them lost to Dutch elm disease. The flowers, though, were his real love. His favorites were poppies, which he first saw as a young lad while working in the oat fields in Denmark. He grew more than 300 varieties of flowers in Minneapolis and loved talking about them to visitors, especially school groups.

For many years he was in charge of Lake Nokomis Park. In those days, he mowed the grass around the lake, using a mower with wide, wide blades that folded up like the wings on a Navy airplane. If something went wrong with the mower, he'd fold up the wings and drive it down Cedar Avenue to the garage on Lake Street, get it fixed, and then drive it back. Can you imagine doing that today?

He also tended the Lyndale Park Rose Gardens between Kings Highway and Lake Harriet and, during his last ten years with the Park Board, was the chief gardener at the Kenwood Demonstration Gardens, also called the Armory Gardens. This was at the corner of Kenwood Parkway and Lyndale Avenue, now occupied by the Sculpture Gardens across from the Guthrie Theater. The thousands of tulips he planted at the Armory Gardens became almost legendary.

He liked planting different things and even put in some cotton plants — probably the only ones in Minnesota — at the Armory Gardens. He got quite a kick out of the reaction of Southern visitors to the sight of cotton. You couldn't make much of a crop out of cotton up here, but at the end of the season he'd bring some home and we'd have cotton balls to show unbelieving friends.

Tens of thousands of people from many states and Canadian provinces visited the Park Board gardens each year. My father became quite well known for his work and occasionally was pictured with his flowers in the local newspapers. He stayed busy in the winter, as well, with the chrysanthemum show at the Park Board greenhouses at 38th Street and Lyndale Avenue.

Except for the soccer he played as a younger man, my father never paid much attention to sports. Even though my parents never influenced me in this area, they gave me every opportunity to develop my own sporting interests.

I was a typical sports-crazy kid and had no shortage of like-minded friends in the neighborhood. My best friend was Don Riley, who later had quite a career as a sports columnist for the *St. Paul Dispatch and Pioneer Press*.

Don and I went to Maria Sanford Junior High together; it was during this time that I began to develop my play-by-play skills. Don—who went on to do a lot of broadcasting, especially of boxing matches, in addition to his writing— also traces his play-by-play abilities back to this time. Along with another friend, Dick Kerr, we started our own dice baseball league.

We would "draft" players—taking turns picking players from the teams in the National League, American League, and the American Association—the minor league that the Millers and Saints played in—until we filled our rosters. I called mine the Long Island Cavaliers (I always thought that sounded classy). We designed uniforms for the teams and even came up with fight songs for them.

Our teams would play games against one another, using two dice. For example, a one and one would be a home run, one and two a foul out, one and three a fly out long enough to advance runners from second and third, etc. We kept statistics—put together complete box scores of every game—but the best part was that we'd get to provide the play-by-play for our team when it was at bat. We'd even call the individual pitches, maybe working the count to three-and-two, then announce what happened, whether it

My mother, Hilda, was as Danish
as my father even though she
never traveled to Denmark.

While I was an only child, we did
have an English bulldog, Lady,
pictured here with my father.

It wasn't fancy, but I made a Minneapolis Millers
jersey out of an old sweater. Mother gave me
the felt, and I cut out the "M".

My good friend Don Riley went into the Army shortly before I did. He's in uniform and I soon would be.

This is in the back yard of our home in south Minneapolis. I spent my first few weeks in the Army only a few miles away, at Fort Snelling.

Our group, on its way home after the fighting ended in Europe, took a 60-franc tour of Paris and stopped at L'Arc de Triomphe. That's me, tenth from the left.

I met Ramona Kinnett while working with the
Radio Guild at KUOM.

I had the chance to interview Bob Hope when I was with KUOM. A fellow
member of the Radio Guild, Duane Zimmerman, looks on.

I spent eight years with WLOL before going to WCCO.

was a single, a strikeout, or whatever.

During one of the games at my house, we had a painter working in another room. At the end of the day, he told my mother, "I've deducted two hours from my pay today. I kept stopping to hear how the game was going."

It was great preparation; it really was. I've often felt— and so has Don—that I couldn't have done a better job preparing for what became my career than what we did for those two summers when I was 12 and 13. (I might add that my son Jim now plays a simpler version of this game, using only one die, with his five-year-old son, Brian.)

My friends and I loved all sports, but baseball unquestionably was number one. We'd often go see the Millers play at Nicollet Park on the corner of 31st and Nicollet, just off Lake Street. Nicollet was a wonderful old ballpark. Left and center fields were deeper than average for the parks in the American Association—the league the Millers played in—but the distance from home plate to the right-field foul pole was only 279 feet. The fence, just a few feet beyond the foul pole, was very tall. There was also a small triangular piece of the roof of the grandstand that jutted out past the foul line and over the playing field. This made it possible for a player, if he could get the ball to land on or even scrape that tiny triangle, to get a home run on a fly ball that had traveled barely 260 feet. It didn't happen very often, but I remember Hub Walker, a Miller of the 1930s, getting two such "shorties" in one series.

Lexington Park, the home of the Saints at University and Lexington avenues in St. Paul, was almost the opposite of Nicollet. Here, left field was the short fence. Behind the fence was the Coliseum Ballroom; many a home run bounced off its roof. By contrast, right field was a long drive. A ball hitting the scoreboard in right-center was a real clout!

There was quite a rivalry between the Millers and the Saints. They'd always draw big crowds for the games between them. The highlights of the season were the holiday doubleheaders played on Labor Day, the Fourth of July, and Decoration Day, which was what Memorial Day was called at that time. They'd have a morning game, starting at 10:30, at one of the ballparks, and then a 3:00 game at the other park. They would alternate. For example, if the morning game was at Nicollet and the afternoon game at Lexington on the Fourth of July, then the morning game would be at Lexington and the afternoon game at Nicollet on Labor Day.

When I began doing baseball broadcasts in 1956, the Saints were still playing at Lexington Park, so I experienced the thrill of calling some games from there. We had a great perch, just above home plate and a few feet back, but the protective screen in front of us had large gaps in it. A foul ball could come back and through that screen, and it often did. I displayed some of my finest fielding while broadcasting there. I never had the chance to broadcast from Nicollet Park, though, since the Millers had moved to Metropolitan Stadium in Bloomington by this time. That was a little disappointing, since I had spent more time as a youth watching the Millers at Nicollet Park. We could get a Millers' ticket at Longfellow Field near my home for either ten cents or a boxtop from Wheaties. My mother would fix me a huge lunch, and my friends and I would hop the streetcars that would take us down Minnehaha Avenue to Lake Street and then over to Nicollet.

All the smokers stood in the back of the streetcar. Even though we certainly didn't smoke at that time (and I never did), we'd stand in the back. There was something special about standing out in the open at the back of the streetcar, holding on to a rail. We'd get to the park early and stand in line off the third-base side on Blaisdell Avenue. I'd have my entire lunch eaten by the time they opened the gates.

When we started going to the games in the early 1930s, the Millers had some outstanding players. Spencer Harris and Art Ruble were in the outfield, Babe Ganzel at third, Leo Norris and Ernie Smith at shortstop, Andy Cohen at second, and Joe Hauser at first. They had an aging, but crafty, pitching staff including Rosy Ryan, Rube Benton, and Jess Petty. The Millers were a Class-AAA minor-league team, only one step away from the majors. As a result we got to watch a lot of players who went on to star in the majors, as well as many who were still hanging on following great careers at the major-league level.

In 1932, the Millers won the American Association pennant and went to the Little World Series where they lost to the Newark Bears, a powerful New York Yankees' farm club that had won the International League pennant.

The Millers didn't win the league championship in 1933, but it was still an exciting year. Joe Hauser hit 69 home runs for the Millers, setting a professional record (which has since been tied and later broken at lower classifications of the minor leagues). A left-handed hitter, Joe was helped considerably by the short distance to the right-field fence. Many of the homers he hit that year, though, would have cleared the fence in any park in the country. Some landed on the roof of the businesses across Nicollet Avenue and bounded into the alley between Nicollet and First Avenue.

A number of other great players spent time with the Millers in the ensuing years. Ted Williams won the American Association Triple Crown in 1938, his last year in the minors before going on to his Hall-of-Fame career with the Boston Red Sox. Willie Mays played for the Millers briefly in 1951. He did so well—hitting .477—that he was called up by the New York Giants only 35 games into the season.

Another player I remember well was Ray Dandridge, who never did get his chance in the majors. Ray was a star in the Negro Leagues and the Mexican League but had most of his good years behind him by the time organized baseball's color barrier was broken by Jackie Robinson. Ray was the most fun of any third baseman I have ever watched. He had this habit of always throwing a runner out by a half-step. He could take a hard one-hopper, look at the ball—seemingly counting the stitches—and then lob it over to first to just beat the runner. On a bang-bang play, though, like a bunt, he'd charge in, scoop up the ball and rifle it to first to beat the runner by half-a-step.

It's unfortunate that, because of his color, he never played in the majors, but at least in 1987, he was elected to the Hall of Fame. I also remember that the Twins brought him back to Minnesota in 1987 to throw out the first ball for Game Two of the World Series. It was a very nice gesture.

I mentioned that I had never broadcast a game at Nicollet Park, but in a sense, I did. Just as I had done with our dice baseball league, I sometimes practiced my broadcasting from the stands at Nicollet Park. Dave Moore—who became the legendary news anchorman at WCCO Television—loves to tell how I'd practice my announcing during Millers games. I got to know Dave when I started at the University of Minnesota. Many of us who worked at the university radio station when we were students, attended Millers games together. I thought it was a good opportunity to hone my skills, but it would drive Dave crazy.

We didn't have major-league baseball in Minnesota during that time, but nobody seemed to care. We were more than satisfied with the baseball provided us by the Millers and Saints.

And then, of course, there was Minnesota Gopher football. The Gophers had some legendary teams in the 1930s under Bernie Bierman. They won national championships three years in a row, 1934 to 1936, and then two more in 1940 and 1941. Bernie recruited many of his players from within the state and often had to go no farther than Minneapolis Marshall High School, just off campus, to find some stars. Babe LeVoir, Bill Garnaas, and Andy Uram all came to the Gophers from Marshall High. Then there was Rice Lake, Wisconsin's Pug Lund, who had such a great season for that first championship team in 1934. And Ed Widseth, from a potato farm in Gonvick in northern Minnesota. Ed played both football and basketball, as well as a year of baseball, at Minnesota. He and his wife, Janet, are two of the most loyal supporters of Gopher sports that the University has ever had. Ed owned a grocery store in northeast Minneapolis for many, many years. People loved him as a grocer and they love him now.

I also remember Bill Bevan, who stood out because he decided to play without a helmet, and later on, Sonny Franck, who could do so many things well. Sonny played on the championship teams of the early 1940s, along with Bill Garnaas, who beat Michigan in 1942 by drop-kicking a field goal, the last successful drop kick ever in the Big Ten.

I followed the Gophers closely and would cut out the game accounts from the "Sunday Peach" section of the *Minneapolis Tribune* and paste them in my scrapbook. Wayne Bell took these marvelous sequence photos for the *Tribune* from the roof of the press box. The pictures would follow one of the key plays of the game with the names of the players superimposed on the picture.

I saw Wayne Bell many years later and told him how much his photos meant to me as a kid. He seemed genuinely pleased that someone remembered.

My scrapbook also included the paper's half-page diagram of the game, a running account of sorts that followed the progress of the ball up and down the field.

When the Gophers were on the road, I'd listen to the games on the radio. When they were home, I attended as many games as I could at Memorial Stadium. Often, I served as an usher at the games. It was a way of getting in to see them.

Those were the glory years of the Gophers and they still stand out, in many ways more so than the years that I spent actually broadcasting the games. Those players were heroes to me.

One of the most vivid memories from my youth involves meeting George Roscoe, a star on the championship football teams from the mid-1930s as well as a fine basketball player at the University. My parents had bought a used accordion for me in downtown Minneapolis. It had no case, so the seller wrapped it in brown paper. We had to take the streetcar home, and the only way to carry the accordion was to put the straps, which protruded out of the paper, over my shoulders. So here I am, with these two straps holding this big mass of brown paper over my shoulder, when I spotted George Roscoe.

"Mother, that's George Roscoe," I said.

"Are you sure?" she asked. I nodded and she said, "Do you want his autograph? Go ask him for it."

So I walked up and said, "Are you George Roscoe?" He said "Yes" and I asked for his autograph.

"Sure," he replied. "Have you got any paper?"

I mumbled, "Well . . . ," and pointed to the brown wrapping around my accordion. He signed the wrapping paper and that's how I got George Roscoe's autograph.

Years later, when he was director of sports for the St. Paul Public Schools, I told him that story. He didn't remember but he got a kick out of hearing about it.

As a youth, I was a much better spectator than player. I went out for football when I started high school at Minneapolis Roosevelt but weighed only 120 pounds and got pretty beat up in practice. I also played baseball in a Sunday league at Sibley Park in Minneapolis. I wasn't a great hitter but I did okay in the field. I didn't have much of an arm so I played second base, where the throws over to first weren't that far.

Sports helped me to make a number of friendships, which transcended the athletic fields. I continued to chum around with Don Riley. I was later an usher at his wedding and he was the best man in 1953 when I got married.

Don and I attended all sorts of sports events together, many of them at the Minneapolis Auditorium in downtown Minneapolis (on the site now occupied by the Minneapolis Convention Center). One of the sports we watched there was the Roller Derby. It was always Minneapolis versus St. Paul, and we'd always root for whichever team was behind in the point standings. Wouldn't you know it—that team almost always won and almost always in the final race!

Then there were the boxing matches at the Auditorium that Don and I attended. We'd buy the cheapest seats and watch the first couple of preliminary bouts from the upper reaches. Then, we'd go downstairs. A door attendant blocked passage to the main floor unless you had a reason for being there (like a ticket for one of the seats). We'd ask for Mr. Olson. The attendant would point him out on the far side (which we knew before we asked). We would start out heading toward Mr. Olson, then veer off to seats in the high-priced section. It never failed.

Don and I also acted in the class play together at Roosevelt. We were in *Pygmalion* by George Bernard Shaw, which later became *My Fair Lady*. Don played Alfred

Doolittle and I was Colonel Pickering. I'll always remember those performances. They were held on a Friday and Saturday night.

The next day the Japanese bombed Pearl Harbor.

Off to War

Pearl Harbor changed everything for us. I graduated from Roosevelt a month later and proceeded with plans to attend the University of Minnesota, majoring in radio speech. Because of the events taking place across both the Pacific and the Atlantic, I knew I'd eventually be going into the service. I managed to get in a couple of quarters, but didn't do any radio work, mainly because I knew I'd be leaving soon.

I enlisted in the Army in April of 1943 and was processed at Fort Snelling. Even though I was there only three weeks, I gained almost ten pounds. They fed you extremely well. I was also allowed to go home at night since I lived so close.

Next I went to Camp Barkley, which was about 20 miles from Abilene, Texas. The closest town was View, although it was hardly scenic. All you could see in any direction was sand. The town consisted of four buildings, including a gas station, a bar, and a small store with a residence on the second floor, which made it a skyscraper.

I played baseball at Camp Barkley, mainly because it got me out of KP and a lot of marches with a full pack. I hit almost .300, which was remarkable for me. (All I saw in the army was fastballs, which I could hit. Anyone with a good curve ball had me at his mercy; fortunately, down there no one had a good curve. It was the one time in my baseball life I was not known as "good field, no hit.")

Then I had an opportunity to go into ASTP, the Army Specialized Training Program at Oklahoma A & M (now Oklahoma State) in Stillwater, Oklahoma. I played a little basketball—very little—but had the chance to scrimmage against Bob Kurland, who was attending A & M. Kurland was seven feet tall and became one of the great big men of his time. He was a monster on defense, stationing himself near the basket and swatting shots away (this was before defensive goaltending was outlawed).

The ASTP folded soon after I got there and I wound up in the infantry, eventually finding myself overseas in Woore in the northwestern part of England.

All I remember about Woore is that everything closed at 8:00 in the evening. It wasn't because of a curfew—we were too far north for there to be any real threat of bombing and there was nothing around important enough to be a target—I think it was just the nature of the town to shut down early.

I was there until June 10, 1944—D-Day plus 4—when we crossed the English Channel from near Bath to Omaha Beach. We had practiced for a month near the small town of Woore. We had practiced climbing down rope ladders as quickly as possible. The ladders would be strung down the side of an LCI, a Landing Craft Infantry. We had practiced running, zig-zagging, through shallow water and on land, just as we would from the bottom of the rope ladders to Normandy beach. We had been shown maps, sketches, a few films of what it would be like once we reached shore. We had been shown where enemy fire was likely to come from—machine guns, 88-millimeter guns, mortar shells, strafing by enemy planes. The only thing we hadn't been prepared for was fear.

The invasion had already begun four days earlier, but somehow that didn't help. We had been told that German forces had been driven inland about a mile, but we had also passed along the horror stories of how men had died. My job was to help transport infantry replacements, replacements for men already killed or wounded in just four days. And that was sobering, frightening, in itself.

I remember sitting, cramped, among other troops and trembling with fear. We were in an LCT, Landing Craft Tank, and we would be able to *walk* out—none of the rope ladders we had practiced on.

It was night, overcast. We were grateful for that. It was damp and cold, but we shivered mostly because we were afraid. It was not just me—it was a group fear. I was relieved that I was not the only one, and yet the fear of not knowing what lies ahead, such a fear shared by many, crowded into a small space, is an uncontrollable phenomenon. There were a few attempts at humor. I tried. So did others. But the laughter was always forced.

I recall thinking that I was not old enough to vote and wondering if I would ever have the *chance* to vote.

It was *after* dawn before we reached Omaha Beach. We would have preferred darkness; daylight was our enemy. We could hear gunfire somewhere inland, but it was a muffled, unreal sound. The beach was quiet—it had been a fairly smooth crossing. We walked—no running, no zig-zagging—straight ahead through shallow water to shore. No machine guns, no mortar or 88-millimeter shells, no enemy planes. And I could feel my fear leave and my muscles relax. It seemed to be a group reaction—almost a synchronized release of tension.

But had our fear been unnecessary? Not for me, I know. I was aware that men had drowned when their craft, often carrying heavy equipment, had overturned in heavy waves—not far from where I walked in a foot or two of water. I knew that men, running zig-zag, had died on the sand where I now walked straight ahead.

I was the fortunate recipient of the gift of time: D plus 4 happened to be immeasurably safer than D-Day or D plus 1.

But the fear I felt, the most complete fear I have ever known, has made me aware, keenly aware, of the incredible bravery of men who preceded me by a day or two or four . . . and I pray that I am a better person *for* that fear and for that respectful awareness.

All the buildings on Normandy had been bombed out, so there was no place to sleep indoors. We had been supplied with sleeping bags and I spent the first night by one of the hedgerows, which were common in the Normandy region. The hedgerows, six feet thick and as much as ten feet high, consisted of bushes, rocks, and dirt that accumulated through the centuries and were used to separate fields. Eventually, we had to use bulldozers and, in some cases, dynamite, to get through them. On this first night, the quiet was interrupted by an explosion. I assumed we were being bombed. For no good reason, I scrambled over the hedgerow and got badly scratched in the process. When I landed on the other side, I realized the explosions were not enemy bombs, but our own anti-aircraft, stationed in the field right next to me. I remember saying to myself, out loud, "You damn fool." I normally don't use profanity, but it seemed appropriate that night.

I was a sergeant, attached unassigned to the 90th Infantry Division of the Third Army—Patton's army. I helped run truck convoys to the forward lines, though not all the way to the front. We'd bring replacements for the wounded and dead. We tried not to think about that, and, fortunately, we didn't carry bodies back. The trucks were usually empty on the return trip.

I had two occasions to see General George Patton. Once was at a distance of three hundred yards when he gave a speech. The other time was much closer, almost too close.

We were taking a break when this jeep screeched to a stop with a cloud of dust next to one of my men, who wasn't wearing his helmet. You always wore your helmet; that was a Patton rule (and a good one). Patton jumped out of the jeep and started chewing this man out. Luckily, he never asked who was in charge, because that was me and I would have been in hot water.

Patton stood nose-to-nose with the soldier and I found out that all the stories of his colorful language were not exaggerated. When he got done yelling, he softened his tone and said, "Don't you think I want you to get home safely?" He then got back into the jeep and they roared away. Believe me, I made sure we all wore our helmets after that.

A few years ago Ramona and I were on a European trip and were able to stop at Patton's grave in the Hamm Cemetery, just outside Luxembourg City. I stood at his grave and saluted. That's usually not my style, but I thought he had earned it.

I ended up in the Battle of the Bulge in Belgium although we were on reserve and never participated in the battle itself. I remember two things. One is that Patton sent out a prayer, which seemed corny at the time, asking God to give us clear skies. The clear skies (which we did receive) really made a difference in our winning the Battle of the Bulge.

The other thing I remember is being quartered in the Belgian home of a large family. They had a radio receiver, which was illegal (not for us but for the family, had the Germans been there). Because of the receiver, we were able to pick up an underground news broadcast out of Norway. I understood enough Norwegian because of my Danish background that I could explain it in French to the woman of the house. She, in turn, explained in Flemish to her elderly uncle. By the time it made it through all these translations, I wondered what story her uncle really heard.

Our convoys covered Germany. We often used the Nuremburg-Frankfurt route. These two cities had been badly bombed, but the downtown buildings were so well built that, although the floors and windows were gone, the walls were still standing. Some were three hundred feet high.

There was a lot of rubble in the streets. People—almost entirely women and old men—would clear the way with shovels and brooms. The Germans actually had some streetcars running. They just kept things going as normally as possible. I admired them for that.

I saw a sign of the Holocaust, a small evacuated concentration camp near the Czechoslovakian border. I remembered hearing how cremated bones were used to fertilize the cabbage plants. We saw some cabbage plants and automatically thought the worst. I don't know if that's how these plants were fertilized, but seeing them was very sobering.

In later travels, we have seen a couple of the larger concentration camps. Auschwitz, in Poland, still has many of the buildings and graphic reminders of the great horror. "Man's inhumanity to man" becomes more than a phrase.

When the war in Europe ended in May of 1945, we had just gotten into Czechoslovakia. Our division was nearing Pilsen but had to draw back. By previous agreement among the Allied powers, Pilsen was to be taken by the Russians.

After the war, I was stationed in Weiden, Germany. My lasting memory is of going to Bayreuth—riding in an ambulance that had some business there—to attend a concert at the Wagnerian Festival House. It was a wonderful evening. The Festival House was a big box-shaped building that was quite new at the time and had not been bombed. In fact, as I remember, Bayreuth and Weiden looked to be in pretty good shape.

Finally, I had enough redeployment points to go home. There weren't enough troop ships, though, so the army held a lottery among all the divisions waiting for homebound ships. Three soldiers from each division were picked for a three-day pass in Paris prior to transfer home. In the 90th Division lottery, my name was one of the three drawn. I toured Paris during the three days and rode the Metro everywhere. It was great!

At the end of the three days, I was taken by truck and then train to the southern coast where we soon were shipped back to the United States. We were hoping to step ashore on Christmas, and we docked during the night between December 24 and 25, but they wouldn't let us off the boat since there wasn't enough room at Fort Dix, where we would be processed. I finally got off the ship on the 26th, was processed two days later, then sent to Camp McCoy in Wisconsin where I was mustered out of the Army on the 31st. I took a train to the Twin Cities, got off at the Milwaukee Depot, and grabbed a streetcar for home, arriving in time to have supper with my folks on New Year's Eve.

It was a wonderful homecoming.

Working at KUOM, both during the time I was a student at Minnesota and after I graduated, was a great experience. That's program director Bun Dawson looking over my shoulder as our producer/writer Bill Connell scans his copy.

Honing the Craft

With the war over, I was able to return to normal life and my studies at the University of Minnesota. I began Winter Quarter at the University in 1946, picking up where I had left off nearly three years earlier.

The University Radio Guild, the student organization that supplied performing talent for KUOM, the University's radio station, and its Minnesota School of the Air, immediately held auditions, which I passed. In addition to that, in May I became a fulltime announcer at KUOM.

KUOM has an interesting history. Radio at the university began as an experiment with the Department of Electrical Engineering in 1912. Two years later, Station 9X1 WX-Z, which it was called then, started formal broadcasts with wireless, Morse Code play-by-play of the Gophers football game against the University of South Dakota. In 1921, it moved into voice transmissions, beginning with weather reports, government information, and occasional concerts and radio plays. The following year, 9X1 WX-Z became WLB, the first radio station to be licensed in the state.

It changed its call letters to KUOM in 1945 and, by this time, had its studios in the basement of Eddy Hall, the oldest building on the Minneapolis campus. It shared air time with WCAL, the St. Olaf College station in Northfield, Minnesota. KUOM had the 770 AM frequency Monday through Saturday, mainly from 10:30 A.M. until sunset.

I officially became chief announcer at KUOM in July. This sounded very important until you looked at our budget, which allowed for one-and-a-half announcers. I was the "one" and my friend Ralph Mauseth was the "half." It was a marvelous combination: I was studying at the University to *become* a radio announcer, and I was working and being paid *as* a radio announcer at the same time.

At KUOM I wrote, directed, acted, and did any number of other things. Much of what we did was live; it was a great experience. We worked some long days but loved every minute of it. And through the Radio Guild, I met my future wife, Ramona Kinnett.

A number of us with the Radio Guild received awards for dramatic programs during the 1946–47 season. I received the best acting award for males and also was recognized for the most service to the station.

I had a chance to do all kinds of roles through the Minnesota School of the Air, a service of KUOM designed to supplement classroom work. We did a number of studio-originated programs for young people. Betty Girling was the guiding light. She understood children's radio better than anyone else I ever knew.

Each May, Alpha Epsilon Rho, the honorary radio fraternity, held a convention in Columbus, Ohio. The awards given were the most prestigious in educational radio. One year, we discovered that KUOM had failed to send in an entry for the kindergarten level. To be eligible, it had to be mailed that day. Betty sat down and, in one hour, wrote "Z. T. Grubney and Spring." I picked the music, played Z. T., and found people to play the other parts and handle the technical needs. We recorded the show in one take and sent it off. It beat the deadline. It won first prize.

We averaged three or four programs a day which ranged from art to history (aimed at a wide age range) to old and new tales (aimed at preschoolers and kindergartners). In addition to Z. T. Grubney, we had characters such as Robert the Tired Rabbit and Freddy the Freight Elevator. Once you've done the voice for Freddy the Freight Elevator, nothing is impossible, so I still do voices when I have the chance. Reading to my grandchildren is the best opportunity. I delight in that kind of silliness; I hope I never lose it.

The other great delight of my time at KUOM was the music. When I became musical director, I began to expand my love for classical music. Some of the records we played came from the personal collection of Burton Paulu, the station's first music director (Burton was the station manager by this time).

I started a program called "The Little Concert," a request program for young people which ran every Saturday from 11:00 to 12:15. The listeners themselves decided what music would be played. Some were from high school, others were younger than that. Often they would band together in making their requests. Instead of playing two minutes of a Tchaikovsky symphony, if six of our listeners got together and requested it, I would play the entire movement. That was great fun. We also formed a group called the Classical Club, so I got to meet many of my young listeners. Our meetings varied from informal concerts by the young people to picnics at Minnehaha Park. When Ramona and I were married, several of the members of the club held a shower for her and many of them attended our wedding in November of 1953.

At KUOM, we also broadcast the Minneapolis Symphony Orchestra's Young People's Concerts, and I experienced the thrill of a live radio concert, a thrill I still feel. When Mercury Records recorded the Minneapolis Symphony, I was permitted to "help." The job was mostly that of a messenger and general handyman, but the producer and chief engineer for the recordings were generous with their time, and I learned a great deal from them.

Long-time listeners may remember other music programs I've done. At KUOM there was "Music for the Asking," an afternoon request program for listeners of all ages, and "A Mood and Music," an hour-long summertime series in which I combined prose, poetry, and music into a "mood." At WCCO I had "Musing on Music," a daily five-minute segment with a short piece of music and its background, and, on Sunday nights from 8:00 to 9:30, "Festival of Music," featuring a variety of selections from Broadway to the light classics.

Today, as I'm known more for my sports announcing, some people find it surprising that I used to broadcast classical music concerts and programs. This perceived incongruity brings to mind the time I interviewed Norman Carol when he was concertmaster of the Minnesota Orchestra (the Minneapolis Symphony had changed its name by this time). We discussed music-related subjects, including Mozart, but also wandered into golf, which was a passion of Carol's. After the interview, I got a call from an irate listener, furious that I had the audacity to permit the subjects of Mozart and golf to be joined in the same interview. I no longer recall whether the caller I offended was an avid Mozartian or an ardent golfer.

If the co-existence of sports and music is seen as unusual, I suggest that it is because the nature of broadcasting, as that of many other professions, is specialization. So many broadcasters are just disc jockeys, or just news reporters, or just sports play-by-play people. The opportunity to achieve diversity is unusual. I have been fortunate, starting out with such an opportunity at an educational station like KUOM and later having the same opportunity for variety at a commercial station like WCCO.

Working at KUOM was not only a tremendous learning experience, it provided plenty of memories of some very funny moments.

I had my share of twist-of-the-tongue accidents. In my first year of broadcasting there, I made this introduction: "It is now my pleasure to *prevent* the Chancellor of the University of Nebraska." Fortunately, the chancellor's address was recorded.

My most embarrassing moment, though, came around that same time, as I introduced a news program. The newscaster, in this case, was broadcasting from a remote location and had no control over his own microphone. I attempted to say, "Now, with the latest local, state, national, and international news, here is . . . " Instead, it came out, "Now, with the *lotest lacal, stote,* national, and international news, here is . . . " When he heard that, the newscaster lost control and started laughing. He laughed through his entire lead story. The worst thing was that the story was about a group of children riding in the back of an open truck that collided with a train, resulting in numerous deaths and injuries. I felt completely responsible because of my botched opening. I have rarely been in such agony.

KUOM was a very proper station, and our audience, we assumed, was very proper also. Certainly profanity would never be a part of anything we did. One afternoon an engineer named Ken Matsumoto was on his hands and knees in our large studio, checking out a problem of some kind. A second engineer decided to play a trick on him. He sneaked into the control room to the studio and, remaining hidden, pushed the talk-back button and bellowed, "What the hell are you doing down there, Ken?"

What the second engineer didn't realize was that the studio was live, and his comment made its way out over our 5,000-watt station—and such a sedate station, at that.

What thrilled me was that we received two cards, not protesting, but asking, "What the hell *was* Ken doing down there?" I realized then that our audience does have a sense of humor. It's a lesson I hope I never forget.

I graduated from the University in 1949 but continued to work full-time at KUOM. I also had the chance to teach, which was indeed a special opportunity to me.

"A teacher affects eternity; he can never tell where his influence stops." Those words by American historian Henry Brooks Adams echo my sentiments as well as those of my family today.

My wife, Ramona, taught high-school speech and English in Rice Lake, Wisconsin, before we were married and in Elk River, Minnesota, after we were married. Our oldest son, Tom, teaches physics at the University of Colorado at Colorado Springs, where he was just named Teacher of the Year. Our whole family has a great respect and appreciation for what teachers can contribute.

I have lasting memories of many of the teachers I've had, especially Dr. Frank Rarig and Dr. E. W. Ziebarth. Dr. Rarig has a building on the West Bank campus named after him. I had a speech class from him, one of the last classes he taught at the University. I've forgotten its title, but I'll never forget Dr. Rarig. He helped me lose many of the inhibitions that exist between the mind and the tongue. He was sharp, and he tolerated nothing but complete attention—and deserved it. Toward the end of a class hour, someone in the extreme front right corner of the room would sneak a look at his watch. Dr. Rarig, looking at the extreme rear left corner of the room, would finish his sentence, pause, then ask, "Does it need winding, Mr. Martinson?"

I actually got my start in teaching as an undergraduate

when I began assisting Dr. E. W. Ziebarth in his General Extension Division radio speech classes. After I graduated and his schedule no longer permitted him to teach those classes, he recommended me to replace him.

This was one area in which I could teach, even though I did not have a degree in education. These were specific classes—Radio Speech, Radio Drama—that students liked so much that they wanted to continue, so the classes were given new titles and new course numbers, and that allowed me to keep teaching these same people, even though they were no longer receiving credit for the courses. Teaching these classes gave me some of the most rewarding hours of my life. There were students of all ages, from teens to post-retirement, and almost all of them had registered for the course because they *wanted to*, not because the course was a prerequisite or required for some other reason.

I wish I could have continued to teach, but my schedule became too full to permit it.

Then, in 1951, a new opportunity beckoned.

I'll never forget those sunny Saturday afternoons at Memorial Stadium.
University of Minnesota

Maroon and Gold on the Gridiron

Fesler and Giel

KUOM was without an announcer for Gopher games as the 1951 season approached. Our program director, Bun Dawson, recommended me to Ike Armstrong, the athletic director, and told him I had quite a background in play-by-play. (If only he had known that this background consisted of announcing games for the Long Island Cavaliers in a dice baseball league.)

The closest I had come to real sportscasting was doing the public-address announcing for the Minnesota band at halftime of the Gopher games. There wasn't much to that. I sat up in the press box, looked down on the field, and read from a script that was given me. I suppose, even from that, I got a little feel for announcing at a football game.

In early September, the athletic director's office hadn't yet announced its decision regarding a new announcer, so I decided I'd better be ready, just in case. For a few Sundays preceding the Gophers' opener, using the only television set in the KUOM studios, I turned on a National Football League exhibition game (with the sound down) and practiced broadcasting it. By the last week in September, I was feeling pretty comfortable about doing play-by-play for football. The problem was, I still hadn't been told if I had the job or not.

Finally, on Monday, September 24, only five days before the opener, I called Ike Armstrong's secretary and asked if they had chosen anyone to do Gopher football. "I've been meaning to call you," she said. "You can't charge over $2.50 per meal for your expenses when you're on the road." With those words, I learned I was going to be announcing Gopher football.

They couldn't pay me anything but expenses, but that corresponded with my fee at the time. I was so happy to be doing the games that I really didn't care about the money. By my second season, though, I was getting $25 a game.

This was the beginning of a new era for Gopher football. Bernie Bierman had retired after the 1950 season. Except for three seasons during the war, he had been at the helm since 1932 and had produced five national championships. He had one of his greatest teams in 1949—with Clayton Tonnemaker, Leo Nomellini, Billy Bye, Bud Grant— although a pair of mid-season losses kept the team from winning the Big Ten title. His final season, following the graduation of those great players, was not a good one. The Gophers won only one game in 1950 and Bernie stepped down.

As pleased as I was to have the chance to broadcast their games, I was disappointed that Bernie would not be coaching. There was still much to be excited about, though.

The new coach of the Gophers would be Wes Fesler, one of the greatest all-around athletes in the history of Ohio State. Fesler had played football, basketball, and baseball for the Buckeyes in the late 1920s. Later he coached basketball at Princeton and football at Pittsburgh before returning to his alma mater to take the head football coaching job in

1947. Under him, Ohio State went to the Rose Bowl following the 1949 season. At the end of the next season, though, Fesler stepped down to go into private business.

The coaching bug was still in him, however, and a few months later he accepted the head coaching position at Minnesota. He had only one starter—linebacker Wayne Robinson—returning from the 1950 team. One of the newcomers of the 1951 squad, though, was one of the greatest all-around athletes in the history of Minnesota sports—Paul Giel from Winona.

Giel was a standout baseball and football player in high school and continued to pursue both sports for the Gophers. He had been a tailback on the football team at Winona, but, for the Gophers, Fesler decided to make him a quarterback.

It should be remembered that football was quite a bit different at that time from the way it is now. The single wing was still being used a great deal. With the single wing, it was the left halfback, not the quarterback, who lined up several yards behind the center and took the snap. The halfback was the chief ball carrier and passer, while the quarterback and fullback were blockers.

The single wing was the primary formation used by Bierman, and Fesler continued with it, although he also made greater use of the T-formation, where the quarterback lined up under the center with the fullback and halfbacks behind him in such positions that the backfield members formed a T.

It would be fair to describe the offense used by Fesler as complicated. He had a lot of different plays. Giel would call the play and, as the team broke huddle and went to line up, it wasn't unusual for one or two players to come back to Paul to double-check on what the play was going to be.

Sometimes Paul was the only one who knew what each man's assignment was.

Another difference was that this was one-platoon football, with players taking positions on both offense and defense. The days of specialization were still in the future for college football.

Giel's first game with the varsity was also my first behind the microphone for the Gophers. The date was Saturday, September 29 – Giel's 19th birthday – and the opponent was the Washington Huskies. Led by their great halfback, Hugh McElhenny, the Huskies had tuned up for the Gophers by destroying Montana, 58–7, the previous week. They were heavy favorites as they came into Memorial Stadium for Minnesota's season opener.

McElhenny scored two touchdowns in the first half and Washington grabbed an 18–0 lead, but Giel was impressive in his debut. He led the offense to touchdowns in the second, third, and fourth quarters to put Minnesota in front, 20–18. The second touchdown was set up by Giel, who had intercepted a pass on his own 18-yard line and returned it 64 yards to the other 18.

The Gophers were on the verge of their greatest upset in years as the clock ran down in the final quarter, and when Bob Thompson intercepted a Washington pass with three-and-a-half minutes left, it appeared they had the game locked away. Unfortunately, Giel was called for pass interference on the play and the Huskies retained possession, getting the ball on the Minnesota 21. Two plays later, McElhenny scored his third touchdown of the game to give Washington a 25–20 win.

Fesler had used mostly a T-formation in that first game, as he did in the next two, which also were losses.

For the Homecoming game against Nebraska, he decided to go back to the single wing. He switched Giel from quarterback to left halfback and the move paid off. Giel ran for 113 yards, passed for 123, and the underdog Gophers pulled off a 39–30 win over the Cornhuskers.

Giel wasn't a bruising runner, the type who bowled over tacklers, and he wasn't blessed with great speed, but he had an elusive quality that made him very difficult to catch and bring down. Appropriately, he became known as the "Winona Phantom."

The greatest run I ever saw *anyone* make was by Giel in the Purdue game that year at West Lafayette, Indiana. The Gophers had fallen behind 19–0 in the second quarter, scored a touchdown to cut the Boilermakers' lead to 12 points, then got the ball back again.

They faced a third-and-12 situation from their own 36 when Giel dropped back to pass. He was hit by three huge Purdue linemen on the far side of the field to my left, 12 yards behind the line of scrimmage. Somehow he got away from these giants, found himself trapped again by other black-shirted defenders, escaped again, and finally broke free. He picked up blockers as he got back to the line of scrimmage and wound up zig-zagging from the far left side of the field to the right side where he scampered down the sideline for a 64-yard touchdown run. If you stretched out the entire route he had run on that play, it would easily have spanned the entire gridiron. Unfortunately, Giel's run completed the day's scoring and the Gophers ended up on the short end of the 19–13 final score.

Because of the Korean War, which was cutting into the available pool of college athletes, freshmen were eligible to play on the varsity beginning in 1951. Giel was a sophomore, however, so he had only three years with the varsity.

What a trio of years it was. He was named the Most Valuable Player in the Big Ten in both 1952 and 1953, as well as being named All-American each year, and helped the Gophers improve from their 2-6-1 record in 1951.

Giel saved his greatest heroics for the Michigan game in 1953, which was the 50th anniversary of the classic game on Halloween in 1903 that started the Little Brown Jug tradition between the two schools.

Coached by Fielding Yost, the "Point-a-Minute" Wolverines (as they were called since they had racked up 600 points in 600 minutes over a four-year period) had not lost a game in more than three seasons when they came to Minnesota in 1903, but the Gophers battled the mighty Wolverines to a 6-6 tie. As the Wolverines returned to Michigan, they left behind a water jug they had purchased that day in Dinkytown. Oscar Munson, a Norwegian custodian who later became the Gophers' equipment manager, took the jug to Dr. Louis Cooke, who headed the athletic department. Legend has it that, with his heavy Scandinavian accent, Munson reported to Cooke that, "Jost left his yug."

Rather than return the jug, Cooke announced that Michigan would have to come and win it back. He painted the words, "Michigan Jug, Captured by Oscar" on one side of it and the 6-6 score of the game on the other, then hung the jug over his desk. It stayed there for six years, since Minnesota and Michigan did not meet on the gridiron again until 1909. The Wolverines won that game to finally get their jug back and it has switched back and forth ever since.

Unfortunately, it has spent far more time in the Michigan trophy case than in Minnesota since the Wolverines have dominated the football rivalry between the two teams. When the teams met in 1953, it had been 11 years since the Gophers had possession of the jug.

A lot was made of the 50th anniversary of the Little Brown Jug. Twelve members of the Gophers' 1903 squad were on hand for the game, but the day belonged to Giel. He carried the ball 35 times for 112 yards and two touchdowns. He completed 13 of 18 passes for 169 yards and a touchdown. But that's not all. He returned a kickoff for 24 yards, four punts for 59 yards, and even intercepted two Michigan passes. It was the greatest single performance I've ever watched in a game. By the time it was over, Minnesota had recaptured the Little Brown Jug with a 22–0 victory.

One of my great disappointments in my years with the Gophers is that Giel did not win the Heisman Trophy, awarded to college football's best player, in 1953. (He would have joined Bruce Smith, who won it in 1941, as the only Heisman recipients from Minnesota.) Paul finished second to Johnny Lattner of Notre Dame. As far as I know, it was the closest margin between the first- and second-place finishers in the history of the Heisman voting.

As good as he was on the gridiron, Giel followed a diamond career upon graduation. He pitched for the New York Giants, Minnesota Twins, and Kansas City Athletics before retiring from baseball in 1961. Two years later, he became sports director at WCCO Radio and, for many years, was my partner on Gopher broadcasts. In 1972, the University of Minnesota named him athletic director, a post he held until 1988. He is now president of the Minneapolis Heart Institute and remains to this day one of the finest gentlemen I have ever met in all my years in sports.

A few other things stand out about those years. In 1952, Gino Cappelletti kicked the only field goal of his college career with the Gophers. It's strange that he kicked only one, because some years later Gino became the best kicker in the American Football League. That same year was also the first season for Bob McNamara, a great running back from Hastings, Minnesota. Bob was later joined by his younger brother, Dick, who was also known as Pinky. The brothers teamed up for an incredible performance against Michigan State on Homecoming in 1954. Bob and Pinky combined for more than 100 yards rushing. They also caught all the Gopher passes that day. For good measure, Bob intercepted a Spartan pass and returned it for a touchdown in a 19–13 win.

By my second season, 1952, I was becoming pretty comfortable in my announcing routine. I was also beginning to earn some respect from my peers and was being recognized as an authority on Gopher football. E. W. Ziebarth, who has meant a great deal to me in my broadcasting career, used me to settle a disagreement regarding a long touchdown pass Giel had thrown earlier that day against Nebraska. The receiver on the play was Jimmy Soltau, who played very little at that time. Somebody at a party claimed someone else had caught the pass. Dr. Ziebarth put an end to the discussion by saying, "If Ray Christensen said it was Jimmy Soltau, then it was Jimmy Soltau." The confidence he had in me was a great boost.

Four radio stations were broadcasting Gopher football when I started announcing. Three of them were commercial stations, and then there was KUOM, educational and non-commercial. In those days, the ratings were measured by a service called PULSE. The commercial stations all paid to subscribe to PULSE, but KUOM didn't. We were always able to find out the ratings, anyway. During my second year of Gopher announcing, WCCO Radio was way out in front in ratings for the games. That was no surprise, but what was shocking was that KUOM was second with more than four percent of the audience. The other two stations, who had around one percent each, protested to PULSE about us. "They're not paying for this service, but you're listing them anyway, and this is hurting us," the stations told PULSE. So PULSE had to list the ratings in a different way. Finally, it decided to list all the non-subscribing stations (of which there was only one, KUOM) on Gopher games as "Other." From then on, "Other" got over four percent of the audience for Gopher football games.

Those early years with the Gophers were great fun. Even though they lost more often then they won, Paul Giel made every game exciting. He graduated after the 1953 season, which was also the last season for Wes Fesler.

Fesler resigned as Gopher coach and was replaced by a man from the South, Murray Warmath.

The Warmath Years

Murray had played at the University of Tennessee under the legendary Bob Neyland in the 1930s and, after a stint as an assistant coach at Mississippi State, returned to Tennessee to serve as an assistant under Neyland. He later was an assistant coach for another legend, Red Blaik, at Army and finally became head coach, back at Mississippi State, in 1952. After Fesler stepped down, Murray was offered—and accepted—the coaching job at Minnesota.

He wasn't well known around here, and some people had trouble with his name. It sometimes came out "Worry Mormath." Soon enough, though, the people got it right.

I came to have a lot of respect for Murray over the years. He endured a lot of criticism when the team was experiencing hard times. The abuse heaped on him in the late 1950s was horrible, but he stuck with it and proved the critics wrong.

In the early going, at least, it was smooth sailing. In 1954, his first season, Warmath installed a Split-T formation offense (similar to a basic T-formation but with a few variations), moved Gino Cappelletti into the quarterback position, and the Gophers won seven of nine games.

They slipped to a 3–6 record in 1955, but one of the wins was a memorable Homecoming game against the University of Southern California in late October. Southern Cal, with its great halfback Jon Arnett, was a heavy favorite, but the elements favored the Gophers. The game was played in a sleet storm. Unaccustomed to such conditions, the Trojans got bogged down on the soggy turf and Minnesota pulled out a 25–19 upset.

The 1955 season was also my last one with KUOM. I had actually accepted a broadcasting position with WLOL that summer, with the provision that I would still do the Gopher games for KUOM. I felt it would be unfair to leave them without a broadcaster, resigning just before the opening of the football season. Fortunately, WLOL was agreeable to me splitting time between stations until the football season was over.

The Gophers bounced back in 1956, thanks in large part to a new quarterback named Bobby Cox. Cox had played a year at the University of Washington before transferring to Minnesota. He was a flashy sort but very good, and he almost took the Gophers all the way to Pasadena.

By this time, I was doing the games for WLOL where I was flanked by two color analysts: Al Gowans, who was the football coach at Minneapolis Roosevelt, and George Svendsen, a former Gopher great.

Having two analysts doesn't always work, but George and Al complemented each other beautifully: they often had differing opinions.

It was quite a year. Minnesota was undefeated heading into the seventh game of the season, against Iowa at Memorial Stadium. The winner of this game would have the inside track toward the Rose Bowl.

There was great interest in the game and nearly 65,000 fans packed Memorial Stadium. However, the Gophers did not play one of their better games. They turned the ball over six times—four times on fumbles and twice on interceptions—and Iowa won, 7-0. Thus, it was the Hawkeyes and not the Gophers who went to the Rose Bowl at the end of the season.

There was disappointment because of this, but with Cox coming back for another season, Gopher fans envisioned great things in 1957. Some people were even taking a Rose Bowl appearance for granted and talking instead in terms of a national championship.

Cox became a national celebrity, appearing on the cover of a number of college football magazines before the season opened. He was even on the cover of *Sports Illustrated*, which has become famous for its cover "jinx." Whether this jinx is real or not, it seemed that the Gophers were jinxed in 1957. The season that started with such high hopes ended up a disaster. The Gophers lost five of their last six games and dropped to eighth place in the Big Ten.

Warmath took a lot of heat for the collapse of the team that year. It got even worse as he attempted to rebuild over the next two years. The Gophers won only one conference game each season in 1958 and 1959, the latter year finishing dead last in the Big Ten.

Some people (I don't want to call them fans because real fans would not do anything like this) started hanging Murray in effigy and even dumped garbage on his lawn. There was alumni pressure on Murray to resign; a number of business leaders even started putting together a fund to buy out the remaining two years of his contract.

On top of the difficulties the team was having winning, Murray was now recruiting on a nationwide basis. The era of the homegrown Gopher was coming to an end. This only added to the ire of some people. They felt insulted that Murray no longer thought the Gophers could win with just local talent, but it was Murray's recognition of this fact that allowed him to plant the seeds for better times ahead. His 1959 squad included a pair of sophomores from rival high schools in western Pennsylvania who would play major roles in the team's resurgence. One was Judge Dickson, a halfback from Clairton, Pennsylvania. The other, from nearby Uniontown, was a quarterback named Sandy Stephens. Stephens was a great all-around athlete and hoped to play baseball in addition to football at Minnesota.

In 1959, Stephens skipped baseball so he could make spring football practice. Murray had promised Stephens he would be free to play baseball in 1960 if he wanted. Following the 1959 season, however, Murray talked to Stephens. He said he would stand by his word of freeing him from spring practice in 1960 so he could play baseball. Then he added that he looked for great things in the next season, and that he would center the offense around Stephens if he would pass up baseball once again so he could practice with the football team in the spring. Warmath's faith in what was ahead rubbed off on Stephens, who agreed to forget baseball and concentrate on football.

In 1960, Stephens was joined in the backfield by a former high-school teammate, Bill Munsey. Another newcomer on the squad that year was Bobby Bell from Shelby, North Carolina. Bell came to the University as a quarterback but before his sophomore year was moved to tackle, a position he adapted to quickly and one that he would eventually play so well with the Kansas City Chiefs that he was elected to the Pro Football Hall of Fame. I must say that Bell looked more like a quarterback than a lineman. Instead of being built like a solid block of granite, as you might expect

52

with a tackle, he had a tapered upper body and a rather slender waist. Whether he looked like it or not, he was a great lineman. Had he stuck with his original position, I have no doubt he also would have been a great quarterback for the Gophers.

Another North Carolina athlete, Carl Eller from Winston-Salem, joined the varsity the following year and, like Bell, went on to star in the professional ranks.

All of the athletes I just mentioned are black. They certainly were not the first blacks to have an impact for Minnesota. In the early part of the century, Bobby Marshall was an All-American for the Gophers. Later, Horace Bell was a member of some of Bernie Bierman's great teams. It was Murray Warmath's recognition of the talents and potential of black athletes that turned his team around.

Many northern schools realized that a great many black athletes in the south were not attending schools in their area because of segregation. By giving these men a chance to play up north, they were also making vast improvements in their teams.

Some black community leaders in the Twin Cities—including Carl Rowan, who was a columnist for the *Minneapolis Tribune* at that time—spoke personally to some of the recruits about why they should come to Minnesota, but the main reason most chose to become Gophers was Murray. Some hesitated at first because Murray was from the south. As they got to know him, they came to realize he was a fair man who cared a great deal about them.

Of course, not all the stars on the Gophers in the early 1960s were black. There was Tom Brown, a defensive lineman from Minneapolis Central High School. Brown had been slowed by a knee injury but came back strong in 1960, receiving a host of honors. He was voted Most Valuable Player of the Big Ten, named All-American, and awarded the Outland Trophy as the best interior lineman in college football. On top of that, he came in second in the voting for the Heisman Trophy. For a lineman to come this close in the Heisman voting was almost unheard of.

After being the Big Ten doormat the year before, the Gophers started the 1960 season by winning their first six games, and found themselves ranked second in the country. The Big Ten's other undefeated team, the Iowa Hawkeyes, had the number-one ranking. They would also be the Gophers' next opponent.

The buildup to this game was unbelievable. Memorial Stadium had been sold out for weeks for the showdown with Iowa, and hotels in the Twin Cities were also booked solid as Hawkeye fans drove up from Iowa for the game.

It was a close contest for three quarters. Iowa took a 10–7 lead midway through the third quarter, but Stephens scored on a quarterback sneak to put Minnesota back out in front before the period ended. Backup quarterback Joe Salem had engineered the big play of that drive, a 28-yard pass to fullback Roger Hagberg, before giving way to Stephens again. Remember that most players still performed on offense and defense. When a player like Sandy Stephens needed a rest, it was just as likely he would get it on offense as on defense. This is why a backup quarterback might come into the game in the middle of the drive. The Gophers put it away with two touchdowns in the fourth quarter, one on a 42-yard run by Hagberg and the final score on a Salem sneak.

The real star of the game, however, was Tom Brown. It was his block on offense that opened the way for Stephens' go-ahead touchdown in the third quarter, but it was on defense that Brown really stood out.

When he attacked, it was something to see. He would hit the line with such force that he'd often drive the offensive linemen back into their own ball carrier. He stopped one Iowa drive by sacking quarterback Wilburn Hollis *without* touching him. He picked up the Hawkeyes' left guard and hurled him back into Hollis, knocking him down. It was Brown's presence that helped set up the Gophers' first touchdown. Iowa had a fourth down from its own 46-yard line and lined up to punt. Intimidated by Brown, the Hawkeye center snapped the ball over the head of his punter. It rolled all the way back to the 14-yard line, where the Gophers took possession. Three plays later, Munsey took a pitchout from Stephens for a touchdown.

Needless to say, after this game the Gophers were the Number One team in college football. That ranking didn't last long. The next week Purdue came to Memorial Stadium and upset Minnesota, 23–14. The quarterback who led the Boilermakers to victory was Bernie Allen, who, two years later, would be playing second base for the Minnesota Twins.

Despite the loss, the Gophers still tied for the Big Ten title with Iowa. Not only did Minnesota get the Rose Bowl bid, but it finished the season ranked as the best team in college football.

Fortunately for the Gophers, the national champions at that time were named prior to the bowl games. In the Rose Bowl on January 2, 1961, the Gophers were defeated by the Washington Huskies, 17–7. Even so, it was quite a year. To go from a last-place finish to a national championship in the course of a year was nothing short of incredible.

Tom Brown graduated following the 1960 season, but many of the star players were back again in 1961. After a non-conference loss to Missouri to start the season, the Gophers won their next seven games. The Michigan game stands out in that string of wins.

Sandy Stephens had gotten married two days before the

game, and Murray wondered what kind of concentration he would get out of him against the Wolverines. Sandy, along with the rest of the team, was sluggish at the start. Michigan had a 13–0 lead when Stephens broke loose on a 63-yard touchdown run in the second quarter. The Wolverines scored again and had a 20–8 lead going into the final period. The Gophers closed the gap on a 46-yard touchdown pass from Stephens and took the lead for the first time on Judge Dickson's touchdown with just over a minute left to play. Michigan marched back downfield, but Stephens preserved the win with an interception near the goal line with a few seconds left in the game.

The Gophers went into the Big Ten finale against Wisconsin looking for an undefeated conference season and another trip to Pasadena. They came up on the short end of a 23–21 score, though, and the Big Ten title went to Ohio State.

It looked like the Gophers' season was over. A few days later, however, the Ohio State Faculty Council voted to turn down the school's invitation to the Rose Bowl. Minnesota would be returning to Pasadena, after all.

This time, the trip had a better ending. The Gophers defeated UCLA, 21–3, on New Year's Day for what remains the only Rose Bowl victory in Minnesota history. It was an appropriate ending for Sandy Stephens' career as a Gopher. He was voted the Big Ten's Most Valuable Player for 1961 and also became the first black ever to be named All-American at quarterback.

(A footnote on Stephens: More than 25 years later, I did the "play-by-play" of a touch football game on Northrop Mall on the University of Minnesota campus. This game featured many former Gophers, including Sandy. He is still built like a barrel, and he still plays to win, while having fun in the process. No matter what the game is, I want

56

Paul Giel and I both began our Gopher
football careers, he as a quarterback and me
as an announcer, in 1951. Later he served as
my broadcast partner for both the Gophers
and Vikings. *University of Minnesota*

I came across this photo of the University's athletic office
early in the century. Hanging above Doc Cooke is the Little
Brown Jug with the score of the 1903 Minnesota-Michigan
game on it.

There are some real legends in this picture. From left, media members Dick Enroth, Halsey Hall, and Sid Hartman talk with past and present coaches Bernie Bierman and Murray Warmath.

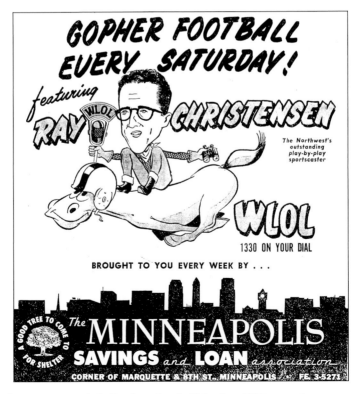

A number of stations carried Gopher football in the 1950s, so there was competition for listeners. WLOL frequently ran ads like this one in the newspapers.

uarterback Sandy Stephens led the Gophers to wo-straight Rose Bowls. They lost the first but won the second. *University of Minnesota*

Tom Brown was one of the most explosive players I ever watched on defense. He dominated the classic game with Iowa in 1960. *University of Minnesota*

This was a great team, the 1960 Gophers, who won the national championship and went to the Rose Bowl. *University of Minnesota*

My broadcast partner, Paul Flatley, and I were the honorary coaches in the 1986 spring game. I'm talking with Matt Martinez at right while Paul goes over the plays with David Williams.

Coach Wacker shared the broadcast booth with us during the 1993 spring game. Sidekick Paul Flatley is at my left with producer Steve Enck behind us. *Photo Jerry Stebbins*

Sandy Stephens on my team.)

In addition to Stephens, Bobby Bell also made the All-American team. Along with Eller, Bell anchored an incredible Gopher defense in 1962. Minnesota posted five shutouts during the season and the Gophers once again went into the season's final game, against Wisconsin, with the Big Ten title at stake.

The game was played at Camp Randall Stadium in Wisconsin, and the Gophers had a 9–7 lead with two-and-a-half minutes left. Then came a play that is still talked about more than 30 years later. Wisconsin had the ball on the Gopher 43. Ron VanderKelen dropped back to pass and was hit by Bobby Bell just as he was releasing the ball. One of our linebackers, Jack Perkovich, grabbed the ball in mid-air at the 37-yard line and returned the interception five yards. It appeared the Gophers had locked up their third-straight Rose Bowl appearance.

Unfortunately, Bell was called for roughing the passer, and the interception was nullified. Not only were the Gophers penalized 15 yards for the roughing, but Murray was so enraged that he got an unsportsmanlike conduct penalty against him. When the officials finally marked off all the yardage, the Badgers had the ball on the Minnesota 13-yard line. They scored a few plays later to take the lead.

The Gophers came back and were aided by three major penalties against Wisconsin, two for pass interference and one for piling on. It almost appeared that the officials were trying to even things up for the roughing-the-passer call. It actually made me more angry to see them do this than the penalty on Bell did. Despite these penalties, the Gophers didn't score. Wisconsin held on for a 14–9 win and went to the Rose Bowl.

The Gophers faced another rebuilding task in 1963, but I wasn't there for most of it. Earlier in the year, I had moved from WLOL to WCCO Radio. Ray Scott, one of the giants of sportscasting, was the broadcaster for Gopher games on WCCO at the time. A national tragedy, however, made it possible for me to do one game that season. The Gophers' last game of the season, against Wisconsin and scheduled for Saturday, November 23, was postponed because of the assassination of President Kennedy the day before.

The game was rescheduled for the following Thursday, which was Thanksgiving. Scott had a commitment to the National Football League—he always broadcast the Green Bay Packers' games on CBS—so I did the play-by-play for the Gophers' 14–0 win over Wisconsin at Memorial Stadium, which also marked Carl Eller's last game as a Gopher.

It wouldn't be my last chance to watch Eller, though. He was taken in the first round of the NFL draft by the Minnesota Vikings and had many great years ahead of him as a member of the "Purple Gang," the Vikings' famous defensive front four.

It was around this time that one-platoon football was dying out in the college game. More and more, teams were going with different players on offense and defense.

The last great two-way player I remember for the Gophers was Aaron Brown, an end from Port Arthur, Texas. He caught 27 passes on offense as a junior in 1964 and almost as many his senior season, when he was named All-American at defensive end. He did this despite playing most of the year with his jaw wired shut. He had his jaw broken in the season's second game, against Washington State, but continued playing. He wouldn't take his helmet off until the game was over, however. He was afraid of what might happen to his jaw if he unsnapped his chin strap. (Murray later told me he wondered why Brown was so quiet at halftime, sitting in the locker room with his helmet still on.)

Following his outstanding career with the Gophers, Brown went on to join Bobby Bell in the defensive line of the Kansas City Chiefs.

The premier team in the Big Ten in the mid-1960s was the Michigan State Spartans, which featured players such as Clint Jones, Gene Washington, and Bubba Smith. The Spartans were undefeated in conference play in both 1965 and 1966. Fortunately for the Gophers, they did not have Michigan State on their schedule either one of these years.

This, combined with the strange no-repeat rule in effect at that time, gave the Gophers hope for another Rose Bowl appearance in 1966. For several years, the Big Ten prohibited its teams from going to the Rose Bowl two years in a row. The Spartans had gone, losing to UCLA, following the 1965 season, which meant another team would have to go the next year.

The Gophers hoped it would be them. They had been pounded, 49–0, by Michigan in October, but since they didn't have to play Michigan State, it was their only conference loss as they prepared to face Purdue in the next-to-last game of the season. Purdue also had only one loss (to Michigan State) and was favored to beat the Gophers, but if Minnesota could pull an upset, then beat Wisconsin in the final game, it would finish second in the Big Ten and get the Rose Bowl bid. It wasn't to be, however.

Purdue came into Memorial Stadium led by its great quarterback, Bob Griese. What I remember most about that game, though, is Purdue's offensive line. This one may have been as good as they ever had. It gave Griese plenty of time to operate, he was able to stay in the pocket and throw strikes, and Purdue went on to a 16–0 win, clinching a Rose Bowl appearance.

With Smith, Jones, and Washington gone to graduation, Michigan State had returned to the ranks of mortals in

1967. The Big Ten's best team was Purdue. Since the Boiler-makers had just been to Pasadena, they would be ineligible to go to the Rose Bowl this year.

It was possible that the second-place team could repre-sent the Big Ten in the Rose Bowl again. The Gophers hoped they could get that bid by finishing in second place. Of course, first place would be even nicer.

They had their chance to do this as they won their first four games of the Big Ten season, setting up a showdown with the Boilermakers in West Lafayette. A win here could mean the Big Ten championship, but once again Purdue was too much for the Gophers. The Boilermakers mauled them, 41–12.

The loss dropped the Gophers to third place, behind Purdue and the other undefeated Big Ten team, Indiana. The Gophers would have the chance to knock off the up-start Hoosiers the following week. Then Indiana would have to finish the season against Purdue—almost a sure loss—while the Gophers could finish up with a much easier game against Wisconsin.

It appeared that the next-to-last game of the season, against Indiana, would determine the battle for second place and an invitation to the Rose Bowl.

Curt Wilson was the hero of this game for the Gophers. Wilson had shared quarterback duties with Larry Carlson the year before. In 1967, these two were joined by Phil Ha-gen and Ray Stephens, Sandy's younger brother. With so many quarterbacks on the squad, Wilson was moved to tailback while Carlson, Hagen, and Stephens shared the signal calling. Midway through the season, though, Mur-ray returned Wilson to quarterback. It paid off right away as Curt threw three touchdown passes against Michigan State in a 21–0 win. In the process, he set a Minnesota rec-ord for passing yardage in a game.

That was nothing, however, compared to what Wilson did to the Hoosiers four weeks later. It was a tight game in the first half. The only scoring came on the opening play of the second quarter as Gophers faced a fourth-and-two from the Indiana six-yard line. Wilson faked a handoff to fullback Jim Carter, but kept the ball and went around right end for a touchdown.

Later in the quarter Indiana drove to the Gopher five, but Del Jessen dropped Hoosier quarterback Harry Gonso for a 10-yard loss. Gonso then had a 15-yard touchdown pass nullified by a penalty that moved them back even farther. After coming so close, all the Hoosiers could do was try a field goal. That fell short, and the Gophers held a 7–0 lead at halftime.

It didn't last much longer. Indiana scored on its first possession of the second half, and the game was tied. The Gophers came right back with a drive of their own. Wilson capped it with another keeper around right end for a touchdown.

In the fourth quarter, it was all Gophers. Wilson ran for his third touchdown of the day. After that Indiana became unglued. On the ensuing kickoff, the Indiana receiver watched the ball drop in front of him, and the Gophers recovered on the 23-yard line. A few plays later, Wilson's fourth-down pass from the 17 bounced off flanker Hubie Bryant's hands at the 5, but was nabbed by right end Charley Sanders in the end zone for a touchdown. It was that kind of a day. Wilson wasn't done yet, though. He ran for still another touchdown, giving him four for the day as well as a touchdown pass.

The Gophers had the ball four times in the second half and scored a touchdown on each possession. The final score was Minnesota 33, Indiana 7. The Gophers were in the driver's seat for the trip to Pasadena.

Indiana was a 14-point underdog in its final game, against Purdue. The Gophers were favored by as much over Wisconsin, which was on the verge of completing its first winless season since 1889. A Gopher win and Indiana loss would give the Gophers the second-place finish that would send them to the Rose Bowl.

Almost lost in all the excitement was the fact that an Indiana win over the Boilermakers, combined with a Gopher win, would put Minnesota into a three-way tie for the Big Ten title with Indiana and Purdue. This wasn't what the people wanted, or expected, however. Such an outcome would send Indiana to the Rose Bowl, since the Hoosiers had never gone before.

The following Saturday, all went according to plan at Memorial Stadium. The Badgers gave Minnesota a battle, but the Gophers seemed in control of the game all afternoon. In the second half, though, we started getting reports from Bloomington, Indiana. The Hoosiers were leading Purdue. Then came the final score. Indiana had won, 19–14.

There was a letdown feeling in the press box. A lot of people had been counting on a trip to California the week after Christmas. Finally, Jules Perlt, the public-address announcer, announced the score to the crowd. In giving the out-of-town scores, Julie sometimes liked to tease the fans by giving the losing score first. This time he played it straight. Now all the fans, as well as players, knew a Rose Bowl trip was out.

Perhaps it was the frustration the Gophers were feeling because of this, but a brawl broke out with two minutes left in the game. I remember the benches emptying and even the cheerleaders from Wisconsin and Minnesota wrestling on the field. After order was restored, the Gophers held on for a 21–14 win.

Ironically, the Indiana victory meant that the Gophers did capture a share of the Big Ten title, but most everyone was disappointed. It seemed the players, the fans, and the announcers would have coveted a second-place finish to Purdue more. As a result, the last Big Ten football championship for the Minnesota Gophers was mourned more than celebrated.

One of the players on that team was McKinley Boston. Twenty-five years later, Boston returned to Minnesota to become men's athletic director. When he was asked about that 1967 season and the strange circumstances that led to Indiana being the Rose Bowl representative, he admitted feeling disappointment at the time but added that now he was happy the Gophers had finished first instead of second, even if it did cost them a trip to Pasadena.

Had the Gophers gone to the Rose Bowl, they would have played the University of Southern California. They got to play the Trojans in their next game anyway. Instead of it being the climax to the 1967 season, it was their opener in 1968. The game was a classic.

It was USC's first trip to Minnesota since that 1955 game in which the Gophers beat the Trojans and their star running back, Jon Arnett, on a soggy field. The conditions for this game weren't as bad, but the field was once again wet from a steady rain that had fallen all morning and into the afternoon. This time, though, the Gophers would have to contend with an even greater running back, O. J. Simpson. O. J. was too good to be stopped by a little (or even a lot of) rain.

Simpson was hampered by the wet conditions initially. The first time he carried the ball, it slipped out of his hands and was recovered by the Gophers on the USC 15-yard line. The Gophers scored a couple of plays later to take a 7–0 lead. They then stopped O. J. again, forced the Trojans to punt, and drove downfield to set up a 40-yard field goal by Bob Stein, putting them ahead, 10–0.

O. J. could be held down for only so long. In the second quarter, he swept around left end for a 36-yard touchdown run. He added another touchdown later in the quarter to put the Trojans ahead 13–10. Another Stein field goal just before the half ended sent the teams into the locker rooms tied, 13–13.

The defenses stood out in the third quarter. The Trojans kept the Gophers bottled up in their own end of the field, while the Gophers came up with big plays to stave off Trojan threats.

In the fourth quarter, Southern Cal retook the lead on a field goal. On the ensuing kickoff, the Gophers tried a play they had spent the previous two weeks practicing. The practicing paid off.

George Kemp took the kickoff at his 17 and headed upfield. After a few yards, he turned to his right and threw an overhand lateral across the field to John Wintermute. The Gophers had set up their blocking on the right side of the field, and Wintermute used that wall of blockers to sail all the way down the sideline into the end zone for a touchdown. Memorial Stadium erupted as Minnesota went back in front, 20–16.

From here on, though, it was all O. J. Simpson. The teams swapped punts on their next possessions with the Trojans taking over on the Minnesota 45. O. J. carried the ball on each of the next six plays. His final run of seven yards was good for a touchdown. He had another seven-yard touchdown run a few minutes later and USC had a 29–20 win.

For the day, O. J. had rushed for 236 yards and four touchdowns. He also caught six passes and returned three kickoffs for 72 yards. It was no wonder he went on to win the Heisman Trophy for that year.

Despite the loss to USC in the opener, the Gophers posted a winning record again in 1968. It was the last winning season for Murray Warmath.

Following a couple of sub-par seasons, Minnesota split its first six games in 1971 but then lost its next four. In the week preceding the season's final game against Wisconsin at Memorial Stadium, there was a great deal of talk that Murray would not be back as coach in 1972. The rumors turned out to be correct.

The players also seemed to sense that the Badger game would be their coach's last and especially wanted to win it for that reason. They trailed by four points, however, with two minutes left in the game. The Gophers had the ball, 80 yards away from the Wisconsin end zone.

With not-to-be denied determination, they moved downfield, and with less than ten seconds left, Craig Curry threw a 12-yard touchdown pass to Mel Anderson for a 23–21 win. As someone who admired Murray Warmath — and I still do, greatly — I was very happy to see that special victory.

Murray later became my broadcast partner for Gopher games. He approached the job of football analyst the same way he took on coaching or any other job. He prepared, and he prepared thoroughly, and he never got too technical with his comments. Both football coaches and everyday fans could understand the points he was making. A special bonus with Murray was his wonderful expressions. "As nervous as a long-tailed cat in a room full of rocking chairs," was a typical one. He must have had a million of these expressions, because he hardly ever repeated one!

Stoll to Wacker

The new coach for the Gophers was an M Man. Cal Stoll had been an end on that great 1949 Gopher team under Bernie Bierman. He went on to be an assistant at Michigan State and a head coach at Wake Forest before returning to Minnesota to rebuild the program. It wouldn't be easy.

Minnesota lost its first five games under Stoll in 1972. For the Gophers' Homecoming game the next week against Iowa, Stoll pulled out a strategy he had successfully used the year before. Using a no-huddle offense, his Wake Forest team had upset Duke. Now he would try the same thing against the Hawkeyes, hoping it might confuse Iowa's defensive scheme. It did. Beautifully.

Gopher quarterback Bob Morgan directed the attack, calling every play at the line of scrimmage. He also listened for the Iowa defensive call. Since the Hawkeyes couldn't huddle on defense, they called out a word to indicate whether the line would charge to the left or the right. Morgan quickly figured out the Iowa signals and would call a play for the opposite direction.

The Gophers rushed for more than 400 yards in the game. Two running backs had well over 100 yards apiece on the ground—John King ran for 173 yards and four touchdowns and Doug Beaudoin had 135 yards while also scoring a touchdown. The Gophers won the game, 43–14, then carried Stoll off the field on their shoulders. Their new coach had gotten his first win.

Minnesota finished with a 4–7 record in 1972, but they turned that record around the following year, winning seven and losing four.

One of those wins—in the next-to-last game of the season may have been the most memorable of all the Gopher games I've broadcast. The Gophers were at Illinois, where they were distinct underdogs.

Minnesota's starting quarterback, John Lawing, was out with an injury. Then, in the week preceding the Illinois game, his backup—Tony Dungy, who would go on to a great career with the Gophers—came up with a mysterious swelling in his passing arm. That left a senior named Gil Fash as the quarterback against Illinois. Fash had labored as a deep backup for three-and-a-half years. He played the role of the opposing quarterback during the week so the Gopher defense could practice, but he never got into the game on Saturdays—not one snap. Now he would have his chance. Needless to say, by this time the Fighting Illini were prohibitive favorites.

The first downs for the game were 20 to 5 for Illinois. Fash completed only two of 12 passes and had four intercepted, but the Gophers had no penalties against them and did not fumble. Illinois, on the other hand, lost the ball six times on fumbles.

One of those fumbles gave the Gophers possession deep in Illini territory late in the game. Illinois tried to cling to its 16–12 lead as Fash rolled out on a perfect bootleg. Twenty bodies piled up near the line of scrimmage. Fash lobbed the ball to tight end Dale Henricksen on the other side of the pile. Henricksen trotted into the end zone and the Gophers had pulled off an amazing 19–16 upset. Incidentally, both Fash and Henricksen were Illinois natives.

The 1973 season was also the first and only year for running back Larry Powell. At the end of the season, he contracted French polio, ending his football career. I've often wondered what the Gopher teams of 1974 and 1975 would have been with Powell and Rick Upchurch in the lineup. Upchurch had two speeds—with fast being the slower of the two. When he shifted gears, it was sudden. Powell had the same type of speed, with great power. They would have been a wonderful combination.

I recall 1977 for a couple of great performances. The first was in the game against Michigan. The Wolverines had trounced the Gophers, 45–0, the year before in Ann Arbor, their ninth-straight win against Minnesota. When they came into Minneapolis in 1977, they were ranked Number One in the country.

The Gophers were as fired up as I've ever seen them for a game. Minnesota kicked off and stopped Michigan cold, forcing a punt. They then drove back downfield and Paul Rogind, a Michigan native, kicked a field goal to give the Gophers a 3–0 lead.

The Gopher defense forced a turnover on Michigan's next play from scrimmage and Minnesota took over inside the Wolverine 15. On a fourth-down play from the 5, Marion Barber—another Michigan native—ran for a touchdown. Rogind's point after made it 10–0.

Rogind added two more field goals, in the second and fourth quarters, to cap the Gopher scoring. All the Gopher points that day were from two players who hailed from Michigan. The Minnesota defense was brilliant throughout the afternoon. It repeatedly pressured the Michigan quarterback, Rick Leach, and did not allow the Wolverines to penetrate the end zone.

The final score was Minnesota 16, Michigan 0. The Little Brown Jug returned to Minnesota for the first time since the Big Ten champion season of 1967. What a feeling it was to watch them hoist the jug high and carry it off the field.

The Gophers may have experienced a letdown after that big win. They lost their next two games and then traveled to Illinois. Once again the Gopher defense posted a shutout, but the big story was the performance of Kent Kitzmann, the big running back from Rochester, Minnesota. He carried the ball 57 times, a national collegiate record, and finished the day with 266 yards rushing, the most for a Gopher runner since 1924. Minnesota beat the Illini, 21–0.

Kitzmann added another 154 yards on the ground in the Big Ten finale against Wisconsin, helping the Gophers to a 13–7 win and a bid to the Hall of Fame Bowl.

It wasn't Pasadena, but it was the Gophers' first post-season appearance since the Rose Bowl New Year's Day of 1962. This time the Gophers traveled to Birmingham, Alabama, just before Christmas to play the Maryland Terrapins. Maryland won it, 17–7.

The Gophers slipped to a 5–6 record in 1978 and Stoll was replaced by Joe Salem as head coach at the end of the season. Salem was the backup quarterback in 1960 who came off the bench to engineer some key drives in that national championship season. He promised a more exciting offense for the Gophers, but it wasn't apparent in the first game of 1979. Even so, the Gophers had little trouble beating Ohio University in Salem's debut.

Their next opponent, Ohio State, would not be as easy. The Buckeyes had not lost to Minnesota since 1966. For this game, though, Salem unveiled the run-and-shoot offense. It used a double-wing formation—players lined up in slot positions on both sides of the quarterback—with one of the wingbacks always in motion before the ball was snapped. This enabled quarterback Mark Carlson to fire volleys in all directions. The wingman in motion could also be a decoy for the sole setback, Garry White.

Operating out of this offense, White rushed for 221 yards in the game. The Gophers scored touchdowns—both by White—on their first two possessions and had a 17–7 half-time lead. The Buckeye defense shut down the run-and-shoot in the second half. Ohio State scored a pair of touchdowns, the second one on a 32-yard keeper by its fine quarterback, Art Schlichter, to take a 21–17 lead in the fourth quarter. Minnesota mounted one last drive in the final minutes. They faced a fourth-and-eight on the Ohio State 43 when Elmer Bailey ran 15 yards on a double reverse for a first down. However, the Gophers couldn't get the big play again. Garry White was stopped an inch shy of a first down on a fourth-down play and the ball turned over to the Buckeyes. Minnesota gave Ohio State all it could handle, but came up just short, losing 21–17.

The Gophers did get a win against Schlichter and Ohio State two years later in what was probably the greatest game of the Salem era. The headlines in this game belonged to the Gopher quarterback, Mike Hohensee. Hohensee threw 67 passes in the game, completing 37 of them for 444 yards. The attempts, completions, and total yards were all school records.

It still didn't look like it would be the Gophers' day, though. They trailed 14–0 after one quarter and 21–7 at the half. A pair of Hohensee touchdown passes tied the score, but Ohio State scored a touchdown of its own just before the third period ended, then added a field goal midway through the fourth quarter to go ahead, 31–21.

However, neither the Buckeyes nor dusk setting in over Memorial Stadium (which had no lights) could stop Hohensee. He connected with tight end Jay Carroll for an 18-yard touchdown to make it 31–28. Minnesota stopped Ohio State on its next drive, forcing a punt, and got the ball back with around three-and-a-half minutes left.

A few plays later, they faced a third-and-ten from the Buckeye 28. Hohensee spotted Carroll in the end zone and fired a pass in his direction. Ohio State's Kelvin Bell dove in front of Carroll. The ball deflected off his hands right to Carroll, who grabbed it for the winning touchdown.

Hohensee later said it was the most thrilling game he had ever been in. I knew what he meant. It certainly was one of the most thrilling I had ever announced.

Two weeks later, the Gophers lost to Wisconsin, 26–21, in what would be the last game ever played at Memorial Stadium. Just a mile-and-a-half to the west, across the Mississippi River, the Hubert H. Humphrey Metrodome was nearing completion.

It wasn't definite at this point that the Gophers would leave Memorial Stadium to play in the Metrodome, but most fans at the game sensed that this was it for the "Brickhouse." After the game, many milled onto the field, some even pulling up pieces of turf as a souvenir.

The Gophers did end up in the Metrodome the following season. Memorial Stadium, which had been their home on campus since 1924, stood vacant for a number of years. A new swimming center was built by the university in the late 1980s inside the walls of the structure on what had been the field. Finally, in 1992, the structure was knocked down. It was sad to see it go. Like so many fans, I have fond, nostalgic memories of the "Brick House." Walking down University Avenue, especially during Homecoming when the fraternity houses all had their decorations, watching the band march by on its way into the stadium— those were marvelous traditions. In reality, though, it wasn't the greatest place for the fans. Over half the seats were beyond the goal lines. For the broadcasters, it was 62 rows straight up to get to the press box. I don't miss that part of it.

The Gophers seemed to take an immediate liking to their new indoor home, beating Ohio University, 57–3, in their first game there. They won their first three games of the 1982 season but lost their last eight.

Things got even worse in 1983. They opened the year

with a non-conference win at Rice, but lost their next ten games. The real low of the season was when Nebraska came to the Metrodome. Led by quarterback Turner Gill, running back Mike Rozier, and wingback Irving Fryar, the Cornhuskers racked up 780 total yards with 585 of them rushing. They scored three touchdowns in each quarter, and beat the Gophers 84–13. Fryar caught only two passes all night, but they were both touchdown strikes of 68 and 70 yards in the first quarter. He had another touchdown on a 41-yard run. Rozier also scored three touchdowns, all of them on the ground, with the last one covering 71 yards.

During the last week of the October, with four games still remaining, Salem announced he would be resigning as coach at the end of the season. A search committee was named to find a new football coach.

For a while it looked like it would be Les Steckel, an assistant coach for the Minnesota Vikings. In early December, Steckel withdrew as a candidate, and the committee had to start over. (Steckel ended up as head coach of the Vikings when Bud Grant stepped down at the end of the season.)

A few days later, Lou Holtz announced his resignation as coach of the Arkansas Razorbacks. Holtz had been contacted earlier by the search committee but asked that he not be considered. Now that he was no longer with Arkansas, the committee decided to try again. Holtz came to Minnesota and met with university officials, including a meeting in a hospital room with athletic director Paul Giel, who was recuperating from heart-bypass surgery. As I recall, Giel told Holtz, "You'd do my heart a lot of good if you would agree to be our coach."

The next day Holtz, despite his hatred of cold weather, accepted the Gopher job.

What an impact this man had right from the start. He revived interest in the football program and was able to get a new indoor practice facility built for the team next to the Bierman Building, the headquarters for the athletic department. The building became known informally as the Taj-Maholtz.

For the first time, Gopher fans began filling the Metrodome on a regular basis for Gopher games. Minnesota improved to a 4–7 record in 1984, and ended the season with a 23–17 upset of Iowa.

Paul Flatley became my broadcast partner in 1985 and I ask nothing more than we continue working together for as long as I continue to do football play-by-play. I had the chance to announce games that Paul played in, from the time he gave the Gophers fits as a receiver for Northwestern to his years catching passes for the Minnesota Vikings.

Paul tells some great stories about his playing days. My favorite is from his college experience. When Paul was at Northwestern, Tommy Meyer was the quarterback, and Paul was his favorite receiver. To help in making the catches, Paul, like other receivers, used "stick-um." Paul not only used it on his hands but well up on both arms.

In a game against Notre Dame, Meyer uncharacteristically overthrew one of his passes to Flatley. Paul realized it was headed beyond him and would likely be intercepted. He leaped as high as he could to swat at the ball to try to drive it off course. In doing so, the ball stuck to his arm!

To this day, it's regarded as one of the greatest catches in Northwestern history.

Paul and I got to broadcast a pair of wins to start the 1985 season. The Gophers then hosted the Oklahoma Sooners, who, with Troy Aikman at quarterback, ended the season ranked as the number-one team in the country. This game came right down to the final play and, while the Gophers ended up on the short end of a 13–7 score, to play so well against a team like the Sooners was nothing short of amazing.

They almost pulled off a Homecoming win against Ohio State, but lost by four points. Even so, they finished with a 6–5 record and received a bid to the Independence Bowl in Shreveport, Louisiana. After a 1–10 season two years before, they were now going to a bowl.

The man who had rebuilt the team, however, would not be with them. Shortly after the regular season ended, Lou Holtz accepted the head coaching position at Notre Dame.

So, instead of Holtz, it was his defensive coordinator, John Gutekunst, who coached the Gophers to a 20–13 win over Clemson in the Independence Bowl. Gutekunst also was named as head coach to succeed Holtz.

In 1986, the Gophers finished with a 6–5 record and another bowl bid. This time they traveled to Memphis, where they lost 21–14 to Tennessee in the Liberty Bowl.

One of the wins in 1986 got the Little Brown Jug back. The game was played in Ann Arbor before over 100,000 Michigan fans. The Gophers led 17–10 in the fourth quarter, but the Wolverines tied it with just a few minutes left. The Gophers moved to just past midfield with time running out when quarterback Rickey Foggie took off on an incredible run.

He went from the far left side of the field across to the near right-hand side. He almost seemed to be moving in slow motion. I remember thinking—at the same time I was announcing the play—if he can get 10 more we'll be in field goal range. He got closer to 20 more yards before he was knocked out of bounds inside the Michigan 20-yard line. One play later, Chip Lohmiller kicked the winning field goal as time ran out.

The 1986 Gophers also had a great running back who

broke in with a splash. Darrell Thompson had 205 yards rushing in his first collegiate game. He was named the team's Most Valuable Player in his freshman season as he ran for 1,000 yards. He had two more thousand-yard seasons, missing a fourth because of injuries. In 1987, he set a school record with a 98-yard touchdown run against Michigan. By the time he graduated, he held the Gopher career marks for rushing, touchdowns, and points scored. He was taken in the first round of the NFL draft by the Green Bay Packers.

In 1989, it looked like the Gophers had a win locked up against Ohio State. Victories against the Buckeyes are something to savor because there haven't been many in recent years.

Until the late 1960s, the Gophers had always been competitive against all teams in the Big Ten. Around that time, however, Michigan and Ohio State began a period of dominance in the conference to the point that it was referred to facetiously as the "Big Two." Starting in 1968, the Big Ten's representative to the Rose Bowl was either Ohio State or Michigan in 20 out of 25 years. The Gophers had as much trouble against these teams as anyone. They had defeated Michigan only twice since 1967. Their record against the Buckeyes was even more dismal—one win since 1966.

They got off to a quick start in this Ohio State game and had a 10–0 lead just 11 minutes into the game. Things certainly seemed to be going the Gophers' way. The Buckeyes drove down to the Minnesota eight-yard line, but then Mike Sunvold hit the Ohio State quarterback behind the line, causing the ball to squirt out of his hand. Defensive back Sean Lumpkin caught it in mid-air and ran it back 85 yards for another touchdown.

Two more touchdowns in the second quarter put Minnesota ahead, 31–0, and it appeared they might get more before the half ended. The Buckeyes had to punt from deep in their territory and the Gophers took the kick around midfield. The way the Gophers were moving the ball, it seemed almost certain they would get another touchdown or at least a field goal before halftime.

Instead, the Gophers were called for having too many men on the field for the punt. The penalty gave Ohio State a first down, and they marched the length of the field, scoring a touchdown and then a two-point conversion with ten seconds remaining in the half.

Instead of going into the locker room with a 34–0 or 38–0 lead, the Gophers were up by 31–8. Up to the point that the Buckeyes scored, I had been completely optimistic. After that touchdown, I started to worry. Who knows what could happen in the second half, I wondered, because Ohio State has always been a good comeback team. On the other hand, of course, 23 points was a very comfortable margin.

Not on this day. Ohio State scored ten points in the third quarter to pull within two touchdowns. I kept trying to remind myself that there was no way a team could blow a 31–0 lead.

The fourth quarter was truly wild. The Gophers added a pair of field goals, but Ohio State countered each with a touchdown to cut the lead to 37–34 with just over three minutes left. They forced the Gophers to punt a minute later, then started a five-play, 73-yard drive that gave them the go-ahead touchdown with 51 seconds to play.

The Gophers weren't done yet, though. They came back downfield and almost pulled it out as a 25-yard pass from Scott Schaffner just bounced off Steve Rhem's fingertips in the end zone on the game's final play.

The Gophers still finished the season with a winning record, but it sure would have been nice to have had that win against Ohio State.

Gutekunst remained as Gopher coach for two more years before stepping down. He was replaced by Jim Wacker, a man with boundless enthusiasm. That enthusiasm is rubbing off on others.

He experienced a tough beginning at Minnesota as the Gophers won only two games in 1992, but they finished the year with a great win over Iowa, coming from behind in the fourth quarter. It was a great way to end the season and look ahead to the future.

I've been around Gopher football too long to start singing "Happy Days Are Here Again," but I like what I'm seeing. Jim Wacker is a good coach, he has a good staff, and he should recruit well.

And maybe, just maybe, there are golden years ahead again for the Gophers.

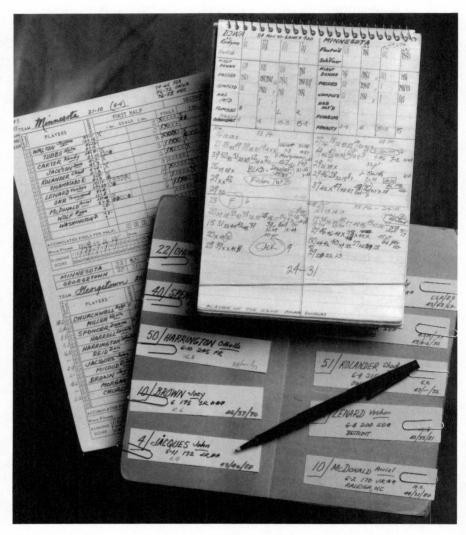

Here are the scoresheets I keep during football and basketball games. The cardboard and paper-clip system in the middle isn't elaborate, but it helps me keep track of the basketball players currently on the floor.

The Art of Play-by-Play

I get a lot of requests from young men (and occasionally from young women) who want to become play-by-play broadcasters. Sometimes they are accompanied by an audition tape or "air check." I always try to answer such requests as well as critique the air checks.

There's really no right or wrong way to do play-by-play. Often what I do is describe my philosophy to sports announcing and tell of my experiences in hopes that there is something to be learned from them.

Throughout the years—no matter what the team or what the sport—I've tried to be fair and objective in my reporting. Sometimes this means being frank, even blunt, in telling it like it is.

On the other hand, I don't believe in all the negative reporting you see today. Every time a play or an individual succeeds, we hear about how someone on the other team did something wrong to let this happen: wrong, wrong, wrong, play after play. In most cases, though, a play succeeds because somebody did something *right*. If a lineman missed making a block that caused his quarterback to get sacked or if a defensive player gets caught out of position, sure, I will mention it. But it's important to remember that, in most cases, a play succeeds because somebody did what he was supposed to do and did it in an outstanding manner. Actually, this extends to my attitude on life in general.

79

Players practice constantly, and what is learned on the practice field is carried over into the game itself.

In this manner, we make our own way in life. It's true of athletic performance, it's true of doing the play-by-play announcing of it, and it's also true of almost anything else in life. If you prepare for whatever you're going to do and approach it with the right attitude, in most cases it's going to come out all right. Fate isn't always kind to us, but we can often guide our own destiny by our day-to-day actions.

My background in radio broadcasting covers more than just sports. In fact, when I started at KUOM (I was a student at the university), I was the music director in addition to reading news and performing in the shows we did. Some shows were dramatic, others of a lighter nature. In the course of this, I learned some valuable lessons about radio that have shaped my style as a sportscaster.

As I took part in writing, directing, acting—as well as coming up with sound effects—for these entertainment-type shows, I began to realize just how visual a medium radio can be.

With television, what you see is what you get, but with radio, if you, the listener, want a man to be tall and slender with a mustache, that's what he is. If you want a woman to be jolly and plump with a terrific smile, that's what she is (but she had better have a smile in her voice). The image is whatever you want it to be. For the listeners, the image becomes whatever they want it to be. Based on what you hear, your mind gives you the picture you want.

So it is with sports. If you're doing play-by-play for a television audience, don't underestimate your viewers' intelligence by describing what they can see for themselves on the screen. Ray Scott, the great sportscaster who has announced a number of Super Bowls for CBS Television, has the right philosophy: "Let the picture supplement your *economy* of words." Ray is known for his economy of words. A touchdown pass from the Green Bay Packers' Bart Starr to Boyd Dowler might generate as few as three words from Ray: "Starr . . . Dowler . . . Touchdown!" On television, viewers can see for themselves what is happening.

Obviously, more description is necessary on radio. You have to supply the "visual." For football, *cuts to the right sideline . . . the ball hits on the 20, rolls to the 15 and is dead at the 12,* or in basketball, *20-foot jump shot . . . right baseline near the corner . . . top of the key,* are visual descriptions. Radio listeners build their mental picture based on what you give them.

Through the years, I've developed my own way of doing things in the broadcast booth. For example, my way of announcing basketball may be unique for a major college play-by-play announcer. I work alone. Actually, there's not a great deal of time for analysis in basketball. Whenever there's a time out, we break for a minute-and-a-half of commercials. Once they're done, there's barely time for any comments before the action begins again.

Football is much different. There is time to fill between plays, and I've been blessed to have a number of good broadcast partners through the years. One thing I've never had is a spotter, someone to help me identify the players on the field. In basketball, a spotter isn't necessary. There aren't that many players to begin with, and you can differentiate between them in other ways besides their numbers. One man is tall, another short; one is black, another is white; one has a brace on his knee, another is wearing goggles—there are any number of things to help set them apart.

In football, though, the players are really upholstered. Even a 185-pound player looks a whole lot like a 240-

pounder from a distance. With football, you have to rely on their numbers to tell who's who. Most football announcers use spotters and use them very well, but if I'm turning to my left or right to see the name of the player the spotter is pointing to so I know who carried the ball or made the tackle, then I'm taking my eyes off the action and falling behind the play. This is why I made the decision to memorize the numbers myself each week instead of having to rely on spotters. It's a lot of work, but it's worth it.

The first game of each season requires the most work, because I have to learn the Gophers' numbers in addition to those of the opposing team. I don't remember their numbers from the year before, and it's just as well that I don't because invariably at least three or four players have changed positions and have a new number. Also, there are always new players on the team. After the first game, I know the Gophers pretty well, so each week thereafter all I need to concern myself with is the opposing team.

I start by typing up the names and numbers of the opposing players. I like to do them at least two deep at each position. For the receiver and backfield positions, however, I go three to four deep.

Just typing all this information starts the memorization process. I then go over the names and numbers, again and again, using a cassette recorder to help me. I record a player's number, name, position—for example, Number 88, Logan, tight end—and then leave a few seconds silent so that as I listen to it I can repeat the information out loud during the silence. The second time through on the cassette, I record only the player's number, so by this time I need to remember that 88 is Logan. I'll start this process on a Sunday and then, during the week, play the recording while driving to and from work.

However, once the game is played the following Saturday, I immediately *forget* all this information. I've spent the whole week remembering who wore Number 44, for example, and now I have to put it out of my mind because a different player for a different team may be wearing 44 in the next game.

I recall discussing this with a young couple from Austin, Minnesota, who were visiting our radio studios during the week before a game. She was a checker in a grocery store (long before products had bar codes which could be passed over a sensitive grid to get a price). She was amazed at the work I did to memorize the numbers until I asked her how many price changes she had to memorize each week. She guessed that it was more than 100. I told her she had a lot more work to do than I did.

In either case, it is hard work, but it's this kind of preparation that makes the game itself relatively easy. If you know how to broadcast a game and have prepared for it, then everything else is done for you down on the field or the court. All you have to do is report it.

I've also done a lot of my own work in keeping statistics, too, but I eventually got a couple of able partners in that department. My oldest son, Tom, started keeping them for me when he became old enough to do so; for the last 15 years, it's been my other son, Jim. They've worked both football and basketball with me, but only for the home games. For all games, I have my own system for keeping a log of what's happened.

In football, I chart every play in a stenographer's notebook. For example, say the opening kickoff was returned to the 24-yard line. On the side of the notebook for the team that has the ball, I write a big "24". They gain two yards running, I write a small "26". An incomplete pass follows and I put an X in the book. They gain nine yards, and I write in a big "35" to show the position of the ball and that it was a first down. I also make a hash mark at the top of the notebook to keep track of the team's total first downs.

If they go all the way downfield for a touchdown, I can quickly count how many plays and how many yards the drive covered. I also write in who scored the touchdown. A "4–Carter" would indicate that Antonio Carter scored from the four-yard line. Of course, the sports information staff is keeping me updated throughout the game on individual totals for rushing, passing, and so on, but I at least have the basics in front of me at all times.

In many ways, I approach basketball broadcasting the same way as football. I always have my opening comments written out. I may or may not use them, but it's reassuring to have them there if I need a "jump start." I also write out my closing remarks. After the play-by-play and the post-game segments are over, it's easy to "slump," and I want the final remarks to say everything they should and to say it smoothly.

Although I can certainly get excited at times, I would describe my play-by-play delivery as low key. I seldom scream and I try not to criticize the officials. The officials have a tough enough time as it is. However, if I feel one of the officials made a call that was incorrect, I'll say so. Whether I think it's good or bad, I'll try to point out the kind of officiating that's present—if they're calling the game closely or letting the teams play. In basketball, more than any other sport, the officiating controls the tempo of the game.

While I have statistical help at home games, I keep track of the most basic statistics myself. When a player scored a basket, I would know exactly how many points he had at that time. I'll also keep a count on turnovers, free throws, fouls, those sorts of things. I don't want to wait until half-time to find out these totals. Sometimes I hear an announcer say of a player, "He must have at least a dozen points now." I've thought, "For Heaven's sake, does he or doesn't he have a dozen points?" It really isn't that hard to keep count.

I also have devised a rather crude, but effective, system to keep track of the players in the game. I print each player's name and number on a card, which I attach with a paper clip to one side of a piece of cardboard. On the right side are five cards, from top to bottom, with the names of the Gophers in the game. The left side contains the opponents. When a substitution occurs, I can easily remove the card of the player leaving the game and replace it with the card for the one entering.

I also include some of the season statistics for that player at the bottom of his card, such as field-goal and free-throw percentage. The latter figure is particularly helpful to know near the end of the game when the trailing team has to foul a player. I can immediately say something like, "They picked the wrong man to foul. This one's shooting 82 percent from the line." (With the advent of the three-point basket in college, I added that shooting percentage to the statistics. Once again, this is important to know near the end of the game if a team has to rely on one of its good three-point shooters.)

When my sons got old enough to handle statistics at home games, it increased the amount of information I could have at my fingertips. First Tom and then Jim began tracking rebounds and shooting percentages as well as scribbling various observations on a notepad in front of me. It's nice to be able to report that "We have 15 rebounds in this game from nine different players."

In addition, I'm scribbling down my own notes. They may or may not turn out to mean a thing. Something may happen and I'll think it could be a turning point in the game, so I'll note the time that it happened and what the score was. If it turns out it wasn't significant after all, I'll cross it out and start something new. Eventually I'll have my wrap—as it's called—when the game is over. I'll have it in front of me just by looking at whatever I haven't crossed out.

All in all, it's a system that works well for me.

I help produce my own games. I have an engineer with me but Steve Enck, the producer, is back at the studio. I call for the commercials when there's a break in the action. If something exciting happens that we can replay on our postgame show, I signal to the engineer to back up the tape and isolate a recording of the play.

During the 1950s, I had the chance to broadcast games in a very different way—recreating the action from the studio as I read a description of what was happening in the game from a Western Union wire. I did this for Minneapolis Lakers' basketball games when the team was away from home as well as for minor-league baseball road games. This was quite an experience and has definitely become a lost art form.

The information came in via a teletype machine, printed out on a continuous sheet of paper. The teletype was four or five steps away from the microphone. I would hurry back and forth between the two, ripping off the sheets from the machine and getting back into my chair behind the mike to describe what was happening.

I found basketball re-creations to be much more difficult than those for baseball. The pace of the game as well as the frequent substitutions made it difficult for both the sender and the receiver. I was constantly encountering a player scoring a basket when, according to the teletype information, he hadn't even entered the game! So, before I could describe the field goal, I had to concoct a situation in which the ball had been knocked out of bounds so this player who is to score the basket could come back into the game. Sometimes it would become ridiculous. We'd have three guys in a row scoring, none of whom were in the game at the time. I really had my hands full just trying to make substitutions.

It also seemed that there were a lot of pretty good *baseball* operators for Western Union, but very few of them had done *basketball*. That led to other challenges, of course. Some of the Western Union operators sent only the sketchiest of details. When a player made a field goal, I might receive nothing more than "FG" with no description of the type of shot or where it was from. This gave me the chance to decide what kind of shot it was. Depending on my mood at the moment, the shots could range from sensational to routine, from sky hooks to long bombs and, on occasion, even a slam dunk. I was enough of a ham to enjoy this opportunity to be creative.

After a while, I found that it worked better if they sent only the essentials. I could communicate over the wire with the operator before the game. He would type material to me and I would answer by typing back. It was all on the same wire that was used when the game finally started. In this pre-game communication, I would tell the operator, "Just give me the things that mean something and the statistics—the fouls, the shots made and missed, the rebounds if convenient. Don't worry too much about anything else."

Some of them still tried to send too much, and it would become a garbled mess. The worst situation was when the Lakers played one of their neutral-site games, this time in Hershey, Pennsylvania, which was a hockey mecca. It seemed basketball was an almost unknown sport to them. My operator for this game had never sent anything but hockey. (How you send hockey I don't know.) I remember that, in the game, he once had the Lakers taking a long shot from the blue line.

(The irony is that Hershey is the city where, a few years later, the game was played in which Wilt Chamberlain scored 100 points. When I noted the dateline over the story of this incredible feat, I wondered if my Western Union operator was relaying an account of it for some announcer elsewhere and, if so, if the operator could really comprehend what he was seeing.)

By the late 1950s, many of the Lakers' road games were being televised. It was against Federal Communications Commission rules to actually use a TV in doing a re-creation. I guess enough years have passed that I can admit that we did bring a television set into the studio with us at times. Instead of reading from a Western Union wire, I could describe the action as I watched it on the screen (although we still made sure the Western Union machine was rattling away in the background). Having the TV wasn't as much of an advantage as one might think. All the electronic equipment in a radio studio played havoc with the television signal, and the picture could be awfully wavy and hard to see. My eyes became bloodshot after a couple of hours of this. I enjoyed doing basketball re-creations, but they could, literally, be a headache.

Baseball was much better suited for this means of transmission than basketball. There weren't the constant substitutions, first of all. If the Western Union operator told me a player had hit a home run, at least I'd know that he was actually in the game. There was an occasional pitching change or a pinch hitter, but it was easy to stay abreast of it all.

I would get a fairly detailed description of what was happening, right down to the balls and strikes. B1 meant ball one, S1C was strike-one called. How about FOGS? No, this didn't refer to low clouds descending on the stadium. FOGS stood for Foul Over Grand Stand. Not all the operators gave that much detail on a foul ball. If they didn't, I could put it anywhere I wanted. I could have it sail back over the grandstand, or have it land in the first row behind the dugout, just out of the third baseman's reach.

We always started our baseball broadcasts for night games on WLOL at 8:00. If the game was in the Eastern time zone, though, it would have begun an hour before we went on the air. On the one hand, this didn't present a problem. I could still re-create the game just fine, even if I was an hour behind, but if we got to 10:00, when the sports shows started on other radio stations, I didn't want these stations giving the final score of the Millers or Saints game when I was still back in the sixth or seventh inning.

What I would do to solve the problem was trim the play-by-play a bit. There were many ways to do this. I had a lot of batters hitting the first pitch. Sometimes, however, it was important to run the count out. For example, if a runner was on first with two out and the batter doubled on a three-two pitch to score the runner, I didn't shave any pitches off. I kept it as a three-two count because it meant the batter would be running with the pitch and could score on a double.

Of course, if a batter walked, I had better describe the three balls that preceded ball four. There were usually ample opportunities to catch up with the action. A long rhubarb would become a short argument. By the time the game had actually ended, I was usually into the ninth inning with my account.

They talk about speeding up the games today. I was an expert at it in my time.

Actually, there were some advantages in having the actual action be a little ahead of what I was describing. It was

nice to have a backlog of wire copy. For one thing, it enabled me to rip off a half-inning of material at a time while
we were taking a commercial break. If we were on the same
time frame, I'd have to hustle to get to the machine and
back to the mike while we were still on the air. We had a
sound effect for crowd noise in the background, so my ab-
sence didn't leave us with any dead air. Even when doing
a game live, a baseball announcer often goes several seconds without saying anything. If the game started at the
same time we went on the air, I would delay things a bit.
If a batter singled on the first pitch to him, I might have him
doing it on a 2–2 count. That way, I could even work in a
couple of extra foul balls to add to the cushion.

We had plenty of sound effects. I would communicate
back and forth with my engineer in another studio to let
him know what I needed. Most sound effects—such as
crowd noise, ranging from loud cheers to boos to just a constant background din—were on records. If we really felt
like being creative, we even had one of a public-address announcer informing the fans of a car in the parking lot with
its lights on.

One sound effect that is needed constantly is the one of
the bat meeting the ball. Broadcasters around the world
have tried to re-create the crack of the bat. I found it by acci-
dent. I was attending a symphony concert when I heard
the drummer's box—a small wooden box that is part of the
percussion section—and I thought, "Gee, that sounds like
a bat." I bought a drummer's box and tapped it with my
pencil. It was a great sound.

Although baseball re-creations usually went smoother
than those for basketball, it didn't mean there couldn't be
problems. Sometimes, for instance, the wire would go
down and our communication would be lost. Usually what
I'd do is come up with a rain delay. (It's a good thing I quit

doing re-creations before domed stadiums came along!) We almost always got the wire back up before too long. Then I'd have the ground crew come back out to remove the tarpaulin.

My most unusual re-creation came when I was broadcasting for the Millers and they were playing the Saints at Midway Stadium. There was a jurisdictional dispute between the managements of WLOL Radio and the St. Paul Saints, and, as a result, we were not allowed into the stadium. I went back to the studio and arranged a telephone hookup with the young man operating the scoreboard. From his vantage point in right-center field (he was actually *in* the scoreboard), he managed to handle his duties of putting up balls and strikes as well as provide me with an excellent pitch-by-pitch description of what was happening on the field. It was the best re-creation data I've ever had.

Re-creations were a team effort among the announcer, engineer, and Western Union operator. When we pulled it off right, listeners might not even know it was a re-creation. I remember the old commercial, "Is it live or is it Memorex?" We had people calling the station, asking essentially the same thing. They wanted to know if I was actually at the game or back in the studio, re-creating it. I considered it a compliment that they couldn't distinguish between the two.

My usual engineer on the night games was Hy Burdman. Hy had a calendar on which he had written "Here, There, Here, There" on alternate dates. He figured he'd average one call per night—usually from a bar—asking if I was here (in the studio) or there (at the game). One night Hy would say, "Oh, he's here." The next night he'd say, "He's there." That way he figured the bar bets came out even.

Needless to say, recreating games provided its share of

unpredictable moments. Of course, the same can be said of broadcasting live from the stadium. Art Linkletter once said, "Kids say the darnest things." So do sports announcers.

Years ago, when Dave Winfield played for the San Diego Padres, he made a valiant try to catch a long fly ball. The play is remembered, not because of his efforts, but because of how it was described by Padres' announcer Jerry Coleman: "Winfield goes back for the ball. He hits his head on the wall. It's rolling back toward second base!"

Even though listeners may have been imagining Winfield's head bouncing toward the infield, Dave survived the play. Coleman survived the fluff.

Fluffs happen to all of us in the announcing business. When Winfield signed a contract with the Minnesota Twins late in 1992, the first thing I thought of was Coleman's broadcast. That opened up a whole cache of memories of fluffs and other inadvertent remarks, some of which I've made.

The one I remember most vividly came when I was doing the play-by-play for the Twins in the early 1970s, shortly before the Washington Senators left the nation's capital to become the Texas Rangers. The Twins were playing the Senators in Washington, and while Herb Carneal was on the air with our broadcast, I went into an adjoining booth where Ron Menzine was doing the play-by-play for the Senators. Ron had a habit of saying that a relief pitcher getting loose in the bullpen was "up and throwing." This time, though, as he looked out toward the left-field corner, he commented, "I see Darold Knowles is throwing up in the bullpen." (Considering the poor support that the Senators' infield gave its pitchers, Menzine's remark may not have been that far off the mark.)

On another occasion, I was doing the announcing of a

Twins game against the Boston Red Sox at Fenway Park. Halsey Hall was seated next to me, providing commentary, when Steve Braun of the Twins fouled a pitch right back into the press box. I found myself saying, "Braun fouls one back our way . . . I've got it!" And indeed I had, trapping the ball as it caromed into the broadcast booth. Halsey looked over and proclaimed to our entire listening audience, "I'll be damned. So you do."

My favorite fluff came from Frank Buetel. Frank, who worked in the Twin Cities for many years, now lives in Florida. When I was broadcasting the St. Paul Saints, Frank was the Minneapolis Millers' voice on WTCN Radio. Frank was describing a pitcher's attempt to hold a runner close to first base: "There's a fast throw over to first. The runner gets back. Another throw. Not much on it this time. Just a half-fast throw."

Frank swears he wasn't aware of what he had said until someone later pointed it out to him. (If you're not sure what it sounded like, read Frank's part aloud.)

One of the players I admired the most during my years of broadcasting
Gopher basketball was Richard Coffey.

Jump Shots

Cowles and Kundla

In more than 35 years of broadcasting Minnesota Gophers basketball, I've seen some great games. The longest one, though, was the game I never broadcast.

It was played on Saturday, January 29, 1955, more than a year before I started doing the games. The Gophers were in Purdue to play the Boilermakers. The squad consisted of three local stars: guard Chuck Mencel from Eau Claire, Wisconsin, and a pair from northern Minnesota's Iron Range—forward Dick Garmaker from Hibbing, and six-foot-eleven center Bill "Boots" Simonovich, who had led Gilbert to the state high school championship in 1951.

When the Gophers had played Purdue in Williams Arena a couple of weeks earlier, it was a high scoring shootout as Minnesota came away with a 102–88 win. This game, however, was much different.

The Gophers played a two-three zone on defense the entire game with big Boots camped under the Boilermaker basket. Purdue countered by playing deliberately on offense, trying to lure the Gophers out of the zone. Remember, there was no shot clock in effect at the time to force a team to shoot. They could hold on to the ball for as long as they wanted, and Purdue went for long stretches in the second half without taking a shot. At the end of regulation, the score was 47–47.

Purdue controlled the jump at the start of the five-minute overtime period and then held on to the ball for the entire period, opting to either win it on a last-second shot or send it into another overtime, which is what happened. The situation was repeated in both the second and third overtime periods. The Boilermakers got the tip, held the ball for nearly five minutes, and missed a shot as time ran out.

Finally, the Gophers got the jump ball to start the fourth overtime. However, Joe Sexson of the Boilermakers promptly stole the ball from Gopher forward Dave Tucker, and Purdue held the ball for a final shot. Once again, they missed.

There was scoring at last in the fifth overtime; each team got a basket. After that, though, Purdue resorted to its earlier form by holding the ball and trying to win it on a shot at the end. Sexson took this shot but it was blocked by Simonovich. Purdue coach Ray Eddy screamed that Boots had put his hand through the bottom of the net and that goaltending should have been called, but the official underneath the basket called it a clean block.

I don't know what got the teams to finally play ball in the sixth overtime. Maybe they just wanted to go home. At any rate, they started putting up some shots. The Gophers were down by three with just over three minutes left when they scored four straight baskets. Guard Buck Lindsley's field goal with a minute-and-a-half to go put them ahead, 55–54. Dave Tucker added two more before the Boilermakers scored at the buzzer (finally making a last-second shot, even though it didn't do them any good) to make the final score Minnesota 59, Purdue 56. The six overtimes tied a college record (since broken).

Garmaker, Simonovich, Mencel, and Lindsley played the entire 70 minutes, while Tucker was spelled for just three minutes by the sole Gopher reserve to see action, Doug Bolstorff.

It was an amazing game in what turned out to be a pretty good season for the Gophers. The two wins over Purdue helped Minnesota to a 10–4 Big Ten record and a tie for second in the conference. At the end of the season, both Garmaker and Mencel were named All-Americans. Since that time, seasons such as this—in which the Gophers contended for the Big Ten championship—were more the exception than the norm. Still, it was exciting.

In the first two decades of the 20th century, the Gophers—coached by Louis "Doc" Cooke—had been a national power in college basketball. There were no post-season tournaments to crown an overall champion, but twice—in 1902 and 1919—they were named national champions by the Helms Foundation.

Williams Arena, even back in its early years, could be a raucous place, and there were a number of great players to watch for both the Gophers and their opponents. The Gopher basketball team first played here in 1928. In fact, James Naismith, the inventor of basketball, was on hand for the event and threw the first jump ball in the facility. Originally, the building was not divided as it is now. Eventually, the west side of the arena became a rink and home to the Gophers' hockey team. That portion of it was renamed Mariucci Arena in 1985 after John Mariucci, a Minnesota hockey legend. (The hockey side is now being transformed into a 5,000-seat pavilion to serve some of the women's teams and smaller-crowd men's sports at the University. The hockey team is moving to a new arena across the street to the north.)

A massive renovation on both sections of the arena began immediately after the 1992–93 seasons. Major work also is being done on the basketball side, which some fans fear will change the atmosphere in the arena. Williams Arena will still have its distinctive raised floor, and I feel it will still get noisy in there and remain an intimidating place for opponents.

My opportunity to be part of Golden Gopher basketball came, although not right away, when I moved from KUOM to WLOL in the middle of 1955. Red Mottlow was broadcasting the games for the station when I arrived, but, after that season, he returned to his native Chicago. I took over the broadcasting duties not only for the Gophers, but also for the Minneapolis Lakers, beginning with the 1956–57 season.

For the first couple of years I did the games, my broadcast location at Williams Arena was at courtside. I don't particularly like sitting courtside in any arena, but at other arenas, you're at least sitting at the same level as the court. Williams Arena has a raised court, which means that press row is down below, with the court at about chest level. As bad as the view is at normal courtside position, this location was just plain awful. Fortunately, I was eventually moved to a perch in the front row of the balcony at Williams Arena, and I've been there ever since. It's much better. From a higher vantage point, you can see what's going on, where the players are moving and whether the defense is a zone or man-for-man. In addition, your view is not blocked by an official, player, or coach.

By the time I started announcing Gopher basketball, most of the players from that classic overtime game with Purdue were gone. I still had the chance to watch, and broadcast, the exploits of Mencel and Garmaker, since they both went on to play with the Lakers.

Of course, there were always new stars to see on the

Gophers. Replacing Simonovich in the pivot was Jed Dommeyer, a fine albeit much smaller player from Slayton, Minnesota. The squad also had an outstanding forward from Dyer, Indiana, named George Kline. Ozzie Cowles, at the helm since the 1948–49 season, was the Gopher coach.

My everlasting memory of Ozzie is that he was a very sharp dresser. He still is. In early 1993, I attended a celebration in the new club room at Williams Arena for Ozzie's 92nd birthday. He was still as natty as ever.

Ozzie was always concerned about mistakes in a game. I remember that he hated it when the Gophers had more than ten turnovers. It's not that unusual now for a team to have that many turnovers in a half. The game is played differently. It's much more aggressive. Teams gamble, take chances. That would have driven Ozzie crazy. His style was to keep the ball moving around the periphery until somebody got open, and then take a shot. Maybe it wasn't as exciting as basketball today, but it usually worked.

The game I remember the most in my first season doing the play-by-play was at home against Iowa near the end of February 1957. Minnesota won the game easily, by a score of 102–81, and George Kline set a new school record with 40 points. He almost didn't get the chance, though. Since the Gophers were so far out front, Cowles substituted for all five starters with about three-and-a half minutes left. Kline had 36 points as he left the game, two short of Maynard Johnson's total against Colorado during the 1950–51 season and one shy of Garmaker's school record for points in a conference game at Illinois in January 1954.

I was aware of how close Kline was to the records, but there was no way I could get word to Ozzie. Fortunately, Otis Dypwick, the university's sports information director, let Cowles know what was happening. Ozzie sent his big forward back onto the court with orders to shoot every time he touched the ball. Kline missed his next two shots but scored on his next one to tie Maynard's mark of 38 points, then added another basket to give him 40 and sole possession of the Gophers' single-game scoring record.

I also remember another game, against Wisconsin, in which Kline had the hot hand. He didn't set any records in this one, but his scoring total was in the 30s. It seemed he just couldn't miss that night. I recall one shot he took. While going up the sideline, he let fly with a hook shot. You have no business throwing a hook up from farther than ten feet from the basket, but George was so confident that he put one up. Cowles buried his head in his hands when Kline took the shot. Then everybody yelled, and Ozzie looked up in time to see the ball go cleanly through the net. He just sat there, shaking his head, not saying a thing.

In one of George's years with the Gophers, the team visited Bloomington, Indiana, for a game with the Hoosiers. Phil Dickens had just been named head football coach at Indiana, and a billboard proclaiming "Indiana Welcomes Phil Dickens" stood near where the Gopher team was staying. Our squad members decided to honor *their* Indiana native, so they secured the necessary paper, paint, and glue, and, the next morning, the billboard read, "Indiana Welcomes George Kline."

One other thing about George Kline. He had a cowlick. I swear that you could tell when George had his shooting touch because his cowlick *bristled*. It was like an antenna. I got the feeling that when his cowlick activated, every shot he took was going to go in. It was kind of a silly feeling, but there seemed to be something to it.

Ron Johnson's first year on the Gopher varsity as a sophomore (freshmen were not allowed to play on the varsity team at that time) was my second season, 1957–58. He had a great career with Minnesota, being named All-American in both his junior and senior years before playing briefly in the National Basketball Association with the Detroit Pistons and Los Angeles Lakers.

The moment that stands out in my mind regarding Johnson came at the end of his outstanding career at New Prague High School. I was broadcasting the Minnesota High School Basketball Tournament at Williams Arena in 1956 when New Prague met Minneapolis Roosevelt in the semi-final game.

This game was an example of having to be careful not to appear partial to either team. In this case, it wasn't hard, even though Roosevelt was my alma mater, because I had such admiration for Ron Johnson, New Prague's center. Roosevelt won the game (the next night they won again to capture the tournament, their first of two consecutive state championships), but Ron Johnson was the fan favorite that night.

When Johnson fouled out with 59 seconds left in the game, the Williams Arena audience gave him the most spontaneous standing ovation that I have ever witnessed. Even the Roosevelt players stood and cheered Johnson as he walked back to his bench. It's still the greatest thrill I've ever experienced with an ovation because it was so natural, so spontaneous.

Minnesota had a new coach to start the 1959–60 season. After 11 seasons directing the Gophers, Ozzie Cowles had been replaced by John Kundla. Kundla had played both baseball and basketball at Minnesota and was a member of the Gophers' last Big Ten championship team in 1937. He began a successful coaching career in the 1940s, serving as an assistant at Minnesota under Dave MacMillan, then taking the head coaching job at Minneapolis DeLaSalle High

School, where he led the Islanders to the state Catholic championship in 1944. After serving in the Navy for two years, Kundla became basketball coach at the College of St. Thomas in St. Paul and then was named the first coach of the Minneapolis Lakers.

Under Kundla, the Lakers won league championships six of their first seven years in existence. The Laker dynasty ended following the retirements of George Mikan and then Jim Pollard in the mid-1950s. In Kundla's last season, 1958–59, he had directed the Lakers back to the NBA Championship Series, where they were defeated by the Boston Celtics. Now he would return to the college ranks with the Gophers.

What a joy it was to work with John. I was already familiar with him since I was covering the Lakers games at the time. With the Gophers, John inherited a team with an 8–14 record and immediately made some improvements.

Kundla's first year was the last for Ron Johnson but the first for two other fine Minnesota athletes, Ray Cronk and Norm Grow.

Cronk, who played in the state high-school tournament three years in a row for Bemidji, became a standout at forward for the Gophers. He was very skinny but had marvelous stamina. Not only was he a great rebounder, but he could lead the fast break upcourt.

Grow had never made it to the state tourney with Foley High School but was one of the greatest players, certainly one of the most explosive scorers, in the history of Minnesota high-school basketball. He started playing on the varsity when he was in eighth grade and ended his career at Foley with more than 2,800 points, a Minnesota record. He set another record his junior year by scoring 70 points in one game.

The six-five Grow had played center at Foley, but was

moved to forward at Minnesota. He never did make the adjustment to the new position and was unable to duplicate his high-school stardom at the college level.

I do remember a funny coincidence concerning Grow early in the 1960–61 season when the Gophers played the Oklahoma Sooners in Norman, Oklahoma. The local Chamber of Commerce had a big drive underway to promote their city and there were billboards all over with the slogan, "Watch Norman Grow." We kept telling Norm that the Sooners were already preparing to defend against him.

In January of 1962 came one of the most amazing individual shooting performances that I have ever seen—certainly that I have had the chance to describe. It was against Minnesota by Jimmy Rayl of Indiana. About two weeks before this game, the Gophers and Hoosiers had played at Minnesota. The Gophers set a team record by scoring 104 points as they beat Indiana, 104–100. In the return match, at Indiana, the Gophers once again scored 104 points. This time, because of Rayl, it wasn't enough.

Rayl was built like his name—a rail. When he pulled up for a jump shot he looked like a pencil. When he was hitting, he was impossible to stop. This night he was hitting.

The game was tied 93–93 at the end of regulation. In overtime, Tom McGrann scored all 11 of the Gophers points. His two free throws with seven seconds left gave him 37 points for the game and the Gophers a one-point lead, but the Hoosiers raced back downcourt and Rayl threw up a desperation 20-foot jump shot that dropped through the basket as the buzzer sounded. Indiana won the game, 105–104, and Rayl finished the evening with 56 points, a new Big Ten record.

Rayl had combined 16 free throws with 20 baskets from the field. This was before three points were awarded for baskets beyond a certain distance in college. It's my guess that at least half his field goals were from beyond today's three-point arc, but in those days, of course, they only counted for two.

The Gophers got a pretty fair shooting performance from one of their own players in the 1962 season finale. Eric Magdanz, a six-foot-six forward from Minneapolis South, broke George Kline's single-game scoring record as he rattled off 42 points against Michigan. The game was never in doubt—the Gophers led by 19 at half and won by a score of 102–80—so the attention late in the game was focused on Magdanz.

He hit a jump shot with just over two minutes to play to tie Kline's total of 40. Around 20 seconds later, he was fouled and sank two free throws to give him 42 points. Magdanz, who scored 30 of his points in the second half, was 16-for-25 from the field and hit on all ten of his free throws. He also had 18 rebounds in the game. It was a great way for him to finish his junior season.

The previous year, his first on the Gopher varsity, Magdanz had what I would call "iron hands." I've never seen quite as remarkable a transformation as the one that took place with Eric Magdanz between his sophomore and junior seasons. He got back the soft shooting touch he had in high school and turned into an outstanding player for the Gophers. Whenever somebody wonders about a Gopher first-year player who doesn't have the shooting touch, I remember Magdanz.

Magdanz and McGrann were joined by a couple of pretty good sophomores in 1962–63: Mel Northway, a center from Minneapolis Henry, and guard Terry Kunze, who had led Duluth Central to the state high school championship two years earlier. Another former Minnesota high-school great on the team was Bill Davis of Richfield.

The six-seven Davis was not only a standout on the

basketball court but a fine baseball player as well. He was a member of Dick Siebert's 1964 national champion Gopher baseball team and went on to play several years in the major leagues with the Cleveland Indians and San Diego Padres.

The Gophers finished 8–6 in the Big Ten and 12–12 overall in 1962–63. In Kundla's first four years at Minnesota, the Gophers had not finished above .500. That changed the following year—the result of Kundla going nationwide with his recruiting.

Like the football team, Minnesota basketball had relied for years on players from around the region. By looking farther, Kundla came up with some outstanding talent. This also integrated the team, as three of the players who were sophomores in 1963–64 were black: Don Yates, a guard from Uniontown, Pennsylvania (Sandy Stephens' hometown); guard Archie Clark from Ecorse, Michigan; and Lou Hudson, a forward from Greensboro, North Carolina.

Hudson, one of the most graceful players I've ever watched, came to the Gophers because many of the major colleges in his area were not ready to integrate. Horace "Bones" McKinney, the coach at Wake Forest University in Winston-Salem, North Carolina, would have loved to have Hudson on his team, but racial policies of the time prevented this. Instead, McKinney called his old acquaintance, Kundla (McKinney had played in the NBA at the time Kundla was coaching the Lakers), and recommended that he recruit Hudson.

The trio made quite an impact right away as the Gophers soared to a 17–7 overall record in 1963–64 and a 10–4 conference mark, only a game behind Big Ten co-champions Michigan and Ohio State. I still maintain that this is the greatest Gopher team I've ever watched, even though there have certainly been other outstanding ones, including the Gopher squad the following year.

In the junior season of Hudson, Clark, and Yates, Minnesota placed second in the Big Ten to Michigan, and finished the year ranked in the top 10 of both the Associated Press and United Press International polls. The Gophers lost only three conference games in 1965, and two of them were to the Wolverines, who had a couple of great stars in center Bill Buntin and guard Cazzie Russell.

With Buntin having graduated, the Gophers had high hopes of dethroning the Wolverines in the 1965–66 season. Their title hopes received a couple of serious blows before they even began their conference schedule. Don Yates was declared scholastically ineligible before the season started. Then, in the Gophers' fourth game of the year, against Creighton University, Hudson was undercut and crashed to the floor, injuring his right wrist. Lou played the rest of the game, finishing with 32 points, but X-rays after the game showed he had broken a bone in his wrist.

With Hudson out of action, Archie Clark really stepped to the front. The Gophers' next game was at Detroit University. Many of Archie's family and friends from nearby Ecorse were in the stands to watch him, and he responded by scoring 38 points in a four-point win over the Titans.

There's no question that the loss of Hudson and Yates hurt. Lou did return to the Gopher lineup on January 15, four weeks after he had been injured, but didn't start a game until mid-February. He had to play the rest of the season with his right hand and wrist in a cast. Even though this hampered his play his final season as a Gopher, I've often felt that the injury turned out to be a fortunate break for Hudson. It forced him to use his left hand more. Hudson was able to gather in some rebounds with his right hand and even put some shots back up with that hand, but basically he became a left-handed player, and a good one. As a result, when he went into the pros, he shot equally well with either hand and thus became virtually impossible to stop. He had an outstanding NBA career with the St. Louis (later Atlanta) Hawks, who retired his number when his playing days were over.

The Gophers finished the 1966 Big Ten season with a 7-7 record, in a fifth-place tie with Northwestern.

They experienced an even bigger drop off following the graduation of Clark and Hudson, finishing 9-15 overall and 5-9 in the Big Ten during the 1966-67 season. One bright spot that year, though, was the play of center Tom Kondla. (People often wondered if Kondla was the son of the Gopher coach. He wasn't, of course; the names were both spelled and pronounced differently. I tried to emphasize the difference in the pronunciation when I said either Kundla or Kondla.)

As a junior, Kondla led the Big Ten in scoring, the first Gopher ever to do so, with 28.3 points per game. He also was named All-American.

Kondla had another great season for the Gophers his senior year and might have had another shot at a scoring title if not for a Big Ten newcomer named Rick Mount. Mount, a six-four guard for Purdue, was one of the greatest pure shooters I have ever watched. He loved to shoot from the corners and, like Jimmy Rayl, spent his college career in the years before the three-point shot. Imagine what his totals would have been had the three-point rule been in effect. Even so, Mount still led the Big Ten in scoring in each of his three seasons at Purdue.

In the late 1960s, I had the chance to watch the Gophers play against UCLA, and their center, Lew Alcindor (now Kareem Abdul-Jabbar), one of the greatest players ever in college basketball. UCLA was in the midst of winning seven consecutive national championships. Kundla tried to prepare his team to play against Alcindor and the Bruins in a tournament called the Los Angeles Classic in December of 1967. In practice, Kundla equipped his players on defense with tennis racquets to try to swat away shots. He hoped this would condition his players to try to shoot over the seven-foot-two Alcindor. I don't think there really was much a team could do to slow down Alcindor on either offense or defense.

UCLA won the game by more than 40 points. The following year, the Gophers again played Alcindor and UCLA in Los Angeles. In this game, at least, they held the Bruins' margin of victory to under 40.

Somewhere along the way during these years, Harvey Mackay told me this story about himself. Harvey was in Des Moines on a cold mid-winter night. He wanted to hear my broadcast of a Gopher basketball game. By opening his upper-floor hotel room window and leaning out with his portable radio, he was able to pick up WCCO.

Now there's a fan. There also is the strongest supporter of Minnesota sports you'll find anywhere.

Fitch-Hanson-Musselman

By the 1968–69 season the Gophers had a new coach, Bill Fitch, who had just come off a very successful year as head coach at Bowling Green State University. Prior to that, Fitch had spent five seasons at the University of North Dakota.

Fitch didn't use tennis racquets to have his team prepare for UCLA in 1968, but a couple of days after that game he found himself having to improvise in practice. They were playing at San Diego State, but when they showed up on campus that afternoon for a practice session, they found the arena locked, and they could not get access to any equipment, not even a basketball. The Gophers did, however, have a lot of tape. So Fitch had the players raid the outdoor, unlocked bathrooms for toilet paper. They wrapped and wrapped the toilet paper in tape until it was approximately the size of a basketball, then, on an outdoor court, they went through a passing drill with that rolled up toilet paper/tape basketball. The "ball" wouldn't bounce, obviously, so all they could do was practice passing. That night, when they played San Diego State, they passed the ball extremely well and came away with a 73–60 win.

In addition to being a good coach, Fitch was quite a character. I often think of a story Paul Presthus tells. Presthus was a star basketball player in Rugby, North Dakota, in the early 1960s and was being recruited by Fitch to play at North Dakota. Presthus, however, finally decided to attend the University of Minnesota. He called Fitch to tell him of his decision. Fitch said, "Wait a minute," and put the receiver down. A few seconds later Presthus heard a gunshot, and then the phone went dead. "My God, he's killed himself," Presthus thought, envisioning Fitch committing suicide over the news that Presthus was not coming to North Dakota. Of course, Fitch was only kidding.

He needed that sense of humor to keep his sanity because he eventually became the first coach for the expansion Cleveland Cavaliers, who lost their first 15 games. (When Cleveland played at Milwaukee one night, Fitch had failed to get a pass to get into the arena. He told the gatekeeper who he was but still wasn't allowed through. Finally, Fitch said, "Look, do you think I'd admit being the coach of the Cavaliers if I wasn't?" The man let him in.)

In Fitch's second year with the Gophers, they came very close to knocking off UCLA at Williams Arena. The Bruins no longer had Alcindor, but they were still a great team and went on to win the NCAA title that year.

The Gophers had Larry Mikan, son of the former Lakers great, at forward along with Larry Overskei and a pretty good backcourt consisting of Eric Hill and Ollie Shannon. Shannon was from Brooklyn but had come to the Gophers as a junior-college transfer after playing at Metro State (now Minneapolis Community College). Minnesota clung to a 68–66 lead in the final minute and tried to run out the clock. With 20 seconds left, Overskei was open underneath the basket, but Mikan's bounce pass to him landed at his feet, skipping through his legs out of bounds. The Bruins came back down and Sidney Wicks tipped in a rebound with 3 seconds left to send the game into overtime.

UCLA scored early in the overtime, then got the ball back when the Gophers missed a shot. They stalled for three minutes before taking a bad shot. The Gophers rebounded, raced back downcourt, and Shannon hit on a jumper from the top of the key and was fouled in the process. There were fewer than 8,000 fans at Williams Arena that day but they almost brought the roof down with their cheering. Shannon stepped to the line, made his free throw, and the Gophers went up by a point. The Bruins' Henry Bibby answered with a field goal, though, to put UCLA back in front. Shannon missed a 20-footer that could have won it in the waning seconds and the Bruins held on for a 72–71 win.

Around this time, I missed a Gopher game at Chicago of Loyola. I flew in the day of the game, but the Chicago airport was completely fogged in. We circled for close to an hour and then turned around and flew back to Minneapolis. I was worried about how the game would get covered, but my engineer in Chicago, Ralph Buehlman, already had things under control. Ralph had heard planes weren't landing in Chicago so he figured he'd better make backup plans. Luckily, being from Chicago, he knew the right people there. He called the broadcaster for Northwestern (located in Evanston, Illinois, a northern suburb of Chicago), which did not have a game that night and asked if he could do the Gopher game. I actually got back to the WCCO studio before the game started and did all the commercials as well as the pre-game, halftime, and post-game shows from Minneapolis. Since that time, I have always flown in the day *before* the game.

Bill Fitch spent two years with the Gophers before leaving to become coach of the Cleveland Cavaliers. He was replaced by George Hanson, one of his assistants who had also played for the Gophers in the 1950s.

Not only did Hanson's team lose its first six Big Ten games in 1971, it didn't appear that the freshman team he had recruited was going to provide much hope for the future. Hanson had given most of the scholarships available to players who had just performed in the Minnesota High School Tournament. None of these players ever played for the Gopher varsity.

One star Hanson did have on his team that year was sophomore Jim Brewer, who had been recruited two years before by Fitch. This was the beginning of rebounding excellence that was very hard to beat. Brewer is still third on the Gophers' all-time rebounding list, and it should be remembered that his totals came in only three years, since freshmen still weren't allowed to play on the varsity team at that time. Shannon and Hill were still on the team (Shannon tied Eric Magdanz's record by scoring 42 points in the Gophers final home game that season). Even with these players Minnesota finished 11–13 overall, 5–9 in the Big Ten, in 1970–71, and Hanson was fired as coach.

In April of 1971, after an extensive search, the Gophers

named their new coach: Cal Luther, the athletic director and basketball coach at Murray State University in Kentucky. One day after accepting the job, Luther resigned as Gopher coach and decided to stay at Murray State. He cited personal reasons for his decision.

Luther finally got his chance to coach at Williams Arena in December of 1992 when the University of Tennessee-Martin, the team he was coaching at the time, played the Gophers. As I watched Luther on the sidelines that night, I couldn't help but wonder how the fortunes of Minnesota basketball might have differed over the past 20 years had he stayed as Gopher coach.

After Luther withdrew, the coaching job went to 30-year-old Bill Musselman, setting off perhaps the most exciting, and turbulent, years in the history of Gopher basketball.

Bill Musselman was a very one-track person. His mind was strictly on basketball and nothing else. My lasting memory of a conversation with Bill is from a couple of years into his regime at Minnesota. WCCO Radio broadcast other sports, such as the Minnesota North Stars, and sometimes there was a conflict if both the Gophers and North Stars played at the same time. Usually, arrangements were made for a delayed broadcast or even to have the game air on another station, but on a couple of occasions, WCCO did not broadcast the Gopher game. Following one of these games, Bill asked me if I had gone to the game anyway, even though I wouldn't have been announcing. I said, "No, Bill, my wife and I went to a concert."

Musselman paused, looked at me, and said, "You know, I wish I wanted to go to a concert sometime."

Prior to coming to Minnesota, Musselman had been the head coach at Ashland College in Ohio, just 20 miles from where he had grown up in Wooster. As a youth, Mussel-

```
MATEOSKY UP BATS RITE
B1 OS   B2 OS    S1S     PTF      PTF
OUT-   MATEOSKY FLIED OUT TO CLINTON IN RITE CENTER.


NO RUNS   ONE HIT  NO ERRORS   ONE LEFT.
SCORE MPLS 1 OMAHA O.



MPLS FIFTH

BOWSFIELD UP
S1S
ERROR- BOWSFIELD BUNTED BETWXXX DOWN FIRST BASELINE. BETHEL
MADE THE PLAYBUT HIS THROW PULLED MATOESKY OFF THE BAG. BOWSFIELD
WAS SAFE ON EXXX ON BETHEL'S ERROR.


PLEWS UP
S1 FOUL ON THE GROUND TO LEFT ON ATTEMPTED BUNT.
 B1 OS PITCHOUT, CANNIZZARO THREW TO FIRST,BOWSFIELD BACK
SAFELY.   S2 FOUL BACK ON ATTEMPTED BUNT.     B2 LO
B3 HI
```

Here's an example of the Western Union transmission I would receive when I did re-creations. See if you can figure out what is happening in this game between the Minneapolis Millers and Omaha Cardinals.

I couldn't ask for better help in keeping track of statistics than I get from my son, Jim.

This is the Gopher team of 1956–57, the first year I broadcast basketball. Ozzie Cowles, well-dressed as always, is in the top left. *University of Minnesota*

I first knew John Kundla when he coached the Lakers. In 1959, he took over as the Gophers' head coach. *University of Minnesota*

Lou Hudson had a great career with the Gophers and then with the Atlanta Hawks in the NBA. *University of Minnesota*

Jim Brewer was the leader of the 1972 championship team. A great rebounder during his playing career, he's now an assistant coach with the Minnesota Timberwolves. *University of Minnesota*

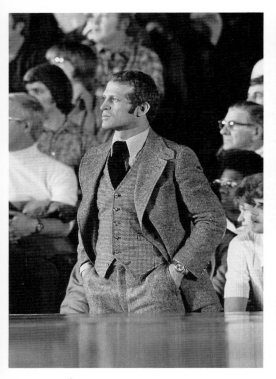

Bill Musselman was as intense as Bill Fitch was funny. He produced a Big Ten championship but also a lot of turmoil in his four years with the Gophers. *University of Minnesota*

Mychal Thompson, the most fluid Gopher I ever saw. *University of Minnesota*

Jim Dutcher coached the Gophers to a Big Ten title in 1982. His earlier great recruiting efforts paid off in the senior season for Gary Holmes, Trent Tucker, and Darryl Mitchell. *University of Minnesota*

Williams Arena is one of the greatest basketball arenas in the country.
University of Minnesota

Clem Haskins started as Gopher coach in 1986 and, within a few years,
brought the team to national prominence. *University of Minnesota*

Willie Burton was a great forward on the 1990 squad that almost made it to the Final Four. *University of Minnesota*

Governor Arne Carlson addresses a celebration at
Northrop Auditorium to honor the 1993 NIT champs.
Carlson is a long-time loyal Gopher fan.

I shared an enjoyable moment at the 1993 Gopher Basketball Awards Banquet.
From left to right: coach Clem Haskins, center Trevor Winter, guard Ryan Wolf,
guard Arriel McDonald, and forward Randy Carter. *Photo: Jerry Stebbins*

All sorts of events took place in the Minneapolis Auditorium. It was here that I broadcast Laker games. *Minnesota Historical Society*

Jim Pollard, Vern Mikkelsen, and George Mikan gave the Lakers the most dominant front line in the NBA in the early 1950s. *Star Tribune, Minneapolis-St. Paul*

man had a pair of good friends from neighboring communities. One was Dean Chance, who went on to win a Cy Young Award with the Los Angeles Angels and later pitched for the Minnesota Twins; the other was Bob Knight, who had just been named the head coach at Indiana University after six seasons at Army.

Musselman stressed defense and, during his first five years with Ashland, the team held its opponents to an average of 39 points per game.

Musselman brought a couple of people with him to Minnesota. One was an assistant coach, Jimmy Williams, who had played for Musselman at Ashland. Another was a player named George Schauer. Schauer played little for Musselman at either Ashland or Minnesota. His function was to lead the pre-game warmup show.

Musselman had started the warmup show, with Schauer the centerpiece, at Ashland the year before. He had his players practice fancy ball handling routines and put on a show for the crowd. When he took the job at Minnesota, he asked Schauer to come with him.

The pre-game show resembled a Harlem Globetrotters routine and was done to the theme song of the Globetrotters, "Sweet Georgia Brown," as well as Schauer's favorite song, "Keep the Ball Rolling." The crowds at Williams Arena loved it.

Musselman added other theatrics to the games that worked the fans into a frenzy. For the introduction of the starting lineup, the lights were lowered with only a spotlight on a wooden cutout of a 17-foot-high Gopher. A couple of curtains covered an opening in the cutout, through which each player emerged as he was introduced.

Musselman instilled an enthusiasm in Gopher fans that remains to this day. For years, Williams Arena had been half empty for most of the games. With the arrival of Musselman, tickets became much harder to get. By his second season, there was so much interest that the University started selling tickets to watch the games on closed-circuit television in the hockey arena side of Williams Arena for people who couldn't get tickets for the basketball side.

When Musselman took over, he let it be known that he had no plans for 1971–72 to be a "rebuilding year." His goal was to win the Big Ten.

To join Brewer, who would play at center, Musselman came up with three junior-college transfers, Clyde Turner, Ron Behagen, and Bob Nix. Another newcomer was sophomore Keith Young. Besides Brewer, holdovers from the previous season included forward Corky Taylor as well as guards Bob Murphy and Roger Arnold, the only seniors on the team.

Soon after the season started, they added another player, Dave Winfield. Winfield had played on the freshman team two years before but then cut back on the sport to concentrate on baseball, in which he was both a star outfielder and pitcher for Dick Siebert. Winfield continued playing basketball, but only for an intra-mural team. While playing on this team he was spotted by assistant coach Jimmy Williams and persuaded to join the varsity.

The Gophers won six of nine non-conference games and, in the process, averaged nearly 11,000 fans at their home games. For their Big Ten opener against Indiana, they had more than 19,000 people jammed into Williams Arena, their first sellout in 12 years.

The conference opener was the first Big Ten game for boyhood pals Musselman and Knight. Like Musselman at Minnesota, Knight had transformed the basketball program at Indiana. The Hoosiers had been picked to finish somewhere in the middle of the Big Ten standings, but, with an 8–2 non-conference record, they were now ranked fifth in the entire nation.

Indiana took the lead late in the first half and held it through much of the second half, but with 17 seconds to play, Bob Nix made two free throws to put Minnesota ahead, 52–51. A few seconds later, Brewer blocked an Indiana shot to preserve the victory.

The Gophers won their next three games and were on top of the Big Ten. Ohio State, at 3–0, was the only other team with an undefeated conference record. The stage was set for the meeting of these two teams at Williams Arena on Tuesday night, January 25, 1972. Another full house was on hand.

The Buckeyes were led by seven-foot center Luke Witte, who was averaging more than 18 points and 15 rebounds a game. Witte made his presence known in the first half of the game in ways that Minnesota didn't care for. The Gophers felt Witte was being too aggressive with his elbows as he went up for rebounds, but the officials were letting him get away with it.

It was a hard-fought first half that ended tied, 23–23. The Buckeyes missed a last-second shot that would have given them the lead at intermission. When the shot bounced off the rim, Bob Nix raised his fist in jubilation. As he walked by on his way to the locker room, Witte slammed his elbow into Nix's face. Television replays clearly show Nix's head being jolted backward as he was hit by Witte.

Ron Behagen started after Witte but was restrained before he could reach him. In retrospect, it's unfortunate that a confrontation did not take place at that time instead of what happened later.

In the second half, Ohio State pulled away in the last ten minutes and held a 50–44 lead with under a minute left when Witte drove in for a lay up. As he went up, he was

115

hit by Corky Taylor and Clyde Turner and knocked to the floor. Turner was called for a flagrant foul and ejected from the game.

Taylor extended a hand to help Witte up, starting a scenario that gave me the most sickening feeling I've ever had in sports. After helping Witte up, Taylor kneed him in the groin and the best way to describe things is to say all hell broke loose.

Witte fell back to the floor and lay there helplessly. Behagen, who had fouled out earlier, came off the bench and stomped on Witte's head and neck until he was finally pushed away by Buckeye coach Fred Taylor. Other fights broke out and even fans got involved. Winfield pummeled an Ohio State player, Mark Wagar, leaving him with a severe concussion. Another Buckeye was injured when he was slugged by a fan.

When order was finally restored, athletic director Paul Giel announced he was calling off the remaining 36 seconds of the game. Ohio State was declared the winner. When this happened, there was an undercurrent of what was called booing from the fans. Ohio State people thought the Gopher fans were booing Witte, but to this day I'm convinced the fans were booing what had happened, that this type of violence didn't belong on a basketball court. They were booing the fact that a game could end like this, in such an ugly manner.

To me, at this point it didn't matter which team I broadcast for. I had just witnessed a brutal assault and that's how I called it. This drew some angry mail from Gopher fans who thought I should be defending the Minnesota players. But this went beyond sports.

Witte and Wagar spent the night in the hospital and each missed a few games because of their injuries. The Big Ten suspended Taylor and Behagen for the remainder of the season. Actually, I was surprised Winfield wasn't suspended as well.

Harsh words flew between Minnesota and Ohio, and the partisan rhetoric served only to inflame matters. The Buckeyes claimed Musselman had "manipulated" his players and that he promoted a "Get Witte" attitude for the game. Witte's father—a professor at Ashland College, where Musselman had come from—added some harsh words of his own toward the Minnesota coach. Even the Gophers' pre-game warmup show was blamed for inciting the fans. There was no shortage of finger pointing.

While I cannot defend the Gophers' actions in that game, I can't find Ohio State completely blameless. A week after the game, *Sports Illustrated* had an article on the brawl entitled, "An Ugly Affair in Minneapolis," in which it painted a picture of the Buckeyes as completely innocent victims. There's no way I can say that what the Gophers did was justified, but there's also no way I can say it was completely without provocation. If you have to misrepresent facts to prove your point, perhaps you're trying to prove the wrong point.

Needless to say, the brawl marred the entire season. It's an incident that many of the people involved have had to live with ever since. It was fortunate that the Gophers did not have a return game at Ohio State that season. It's hard to imagine how tense that game would have been.

A postscript on the incident. I later heard from a couple of Minnesota students who had sent letters that had been critical of how I described what had happened. They both said they had been wrong, that they hadn't realized the extent of what had gone on. I really appreciated them taking the time to write back. I also received some phone calls, and most were complimentary. I was amazed to hear from sports information directors from three different schools in the Big Ten. Since both teams were undefeated, there was great interest in the game. The three who contacted me all had nice things to say about how I handled it.

We could feel the tension as Minnesota played on the road the rest of the season. The Gophers were not popular in opposing arenas because of what had happened. I remember the fans on the road as still being very fair. The next game after the brawl was in Iowa, which could be an unfriendly place for visitors even under normal circumstances. As the Gophers came on the floor and the Iowa public-address announcer made his usual announcement, "Let's give a warm welcome to our guests from the University of Minnesota," the fans applauded. It wasn't a standing ovation by any means, but they were very polite.

The Gophers went on to win that game. The suspensions of Behagen and Taylor left the Gophers shorthanded, but their "Iron Five" of Dave Winfield, Clyde Turner, Jim Brewer, Bob Nix, and Keith Young carried on. They lost a few, but won more than I would have expected after all that had happened, and by the end of February, they were tied for the Big Ten lead with Ohio State.

The following Saturday the Gophers beat Illinois in their final home game at the same time that Ohio State was losing. The Gophers had clinched a tie for the Big Ten title and could capture their first outright conference championship since 1919 with a win the next week at Purdue. If they lost and finished in a first-place tie, a playoff game at a neutral site would have to be held to determine the Big Ten representative to the NCAA tournament. (Far fewer teams went to the NCAA tournament then than do now.)

The Gophers appeared to have the game easily in hand as they opened up a 15-point lead midway through the second half, but Minnesota didn't get off a shot from the field for the final eight minutes and the Boilermakers whittled away at the lead.

The Gophers clung to a 49–48 lead, but Purdue had the ball with 13 seconds left. They got off three shots before time ran out, but all missed the mark. Musselman later called it "the longest 13 seconds in history."

So the Gophers were Big Ten champions and prepared for the first post-season appearance in their history. For the first round of the NCAA tournament, they were matched against Florida State in a game to be played in Dayton, Ohio.

Remembering what had happened against the Buckeyes, the Ohio fans definitely were not on the side of the Gophers. However, it wasn't the fans as much as it was the huge front line of the Florida State Seminoles that bothered the Gophers as they went down to defeat, 70–56. A couple of days later, the Gophers beat Marquette University in a consolation game, finally bringing to an end a most tumultuous season.

Behagen and Taylor were back for the 1972–73 season, as were the "Iron Five." They had a perfect non-conference season and then won 10 of their first 12 conference games to put them on the verge of another Big Ten title. Their final two games were against the bottom two teams in the conference, Iowa and Northwestern. Wins in both games would clinch the championship. One win would clinch a tie and at least force a playoff for the NCAA tournament spot.

The game against Iowa was also the final home game of the season. At halftime, the Gophers brought Jim Brewer back onto the court to retire his number 52. It was the first Minnesota basketball number ever retired. Things looked pretty good at that time as the Gophers held a 46–33 lead.

Iowa came back strong in the second half. They took the

lead late in the game, but Brewer put Minnesota back on top by a point with 36 seconds left. The Hawkeyes then ran the clock down, looking to win on a shot in the closing seconds. They got the ball to their seven-foot center, Kevin Kunnert, who put up a shot that was blocked by Brewer under the basket, but the ball came back to Kunnert, who shoveled it into the basket to win the game for Iowa.

Now the Gophers would have to win at Northwestern to at least finish in a first-place tie. The Wildcats had won only one game all year so a Gopher victory appeared to be a foregone conclusion. It didn't work out that way. Northwestern won, 79–74, to knock Minnesota out of first place. The Big Ten title went instead to Indiana.

The Gophers dropped to a 12–12 record the next season as most of their starters had graduated, but they came back strong in 1974–75. By this time, freshmen were eligible for the varsity and Minnesota had quite a freshman crop, including two players originally from the Bahamas who had played high-school ball together in Miami. One was guard Osborne "Goose" Lockhart and the other a six-foot-ten center, Mike Thompson. (Thompson's original name was Michael. Before he finished his great career at Minnesota, he had changed it to Mychal.)

The Gophers had a pair of local Marks in the front court. Mark Landsberger, a standout at Mounds View High School, had transferred to Minnesota after a year at a junior college in California. He was joined by freshman Mark Olberding, who had just led Melrose High School to the state championship. Unfortunately, this was the only year for both players at Minnesota. Landsberger transferred again, this time to Arizona State, while Olberding signed a pro contract following his freshman season. I know it's useless to speculate on what might have been, but I still think back to how great the Gophers could have been had Olberding and Landsberger stayed.

This was also the final year for Bill Musselman with the Gophers. He accepted a coaching position with the San Diego Sails of the American Basketball Association following the 1974–75 season and left Minnesota at the same time the basketball program was being charged with more than 100 violations by the NCAA.

I still remember Musselman's parting words: "The investigation is of the University, not a single individual. And I am no longer a member of the University of Minnesota."

Dutcher and Haskins

It would be left to another coach to bear the burden of the penalties that would be assessed by the NCAA. That coach was to be Jim Dutcher. He had been an assistant coach for the Michigan Wolverines for the past three seasons and head coach at Eastern Michigan University for six years before that.

Even though the eventual NCAA sanctions left the basketball program short on scholarships and ineligible for post-season tournaments for three years, Dutcher continued to build the program.

He added an outstanding guard, Ray Williams, a junior-college transfer. What a backcourt Williams and Lockhart gave the Gophers. I especially remember when the pair would fast break together. Ray would get a grin on his face, and it would get wider and wider in the split seconds that it took for them to go from one end of the court to the other. Whether it was he or Lockhart who got the basket, by the

121

time that ball went into the hoop, Williams' grin was wall to wall. It was fun.

Another fine guard the Gophers had around this time was Phil "Flip" Saunders, who was like a coach on the floor. He ran the team extremely well. So the team was far more than Mychal Thompson. Mychal, though, was the most fluid Gopher I have ever seen play. With a great touch on his turnaround jumpers, he was nearly impossible to stop when he got the ball down low. By his junior season, Thompson was joined by Kevin McHale, out of Hibbing High School. Kevin had a great career with the Gophers and went on to an even greater one with the Boston Celtics. Thompson was named All-American in both 1977 and 1978 and was the first player taken in the NBA draft, by the Portland Trail Blazers.

The Gophers won 24 games during the 1976–77 season, their most ever. They were 15–3 in conference play, finishing second in the Big Ten to Michigan. They tied for second in the conference the following season. Unfortunately, they were still ineligible for post-season play. By this time, the NCAA had increased the number of teams invited to its tournament. If not for the sanctions against them, it's likely the Gophers would have been in the NCAA tournament both seasons.

The mid-1970s brought the best opposing team I've ever seen in the Big Ten, the Indiana Hoosiers. The 1975 conference season was the first in which all teams played each other twice, once at home and once on the road. Indiana finished with an 18–0 record in the Big Ten that year. They had another 18–0 season in 1976 on the way to winning their first national championship under Bobby Knight. The Hoosiers were led by Scott May, perhaps the finest all-around player I have ever watched play on a regular basis. The only other player I could compare with May was Earvin "Magic" Johnson, who came along a couple of years later. But that Indiana team — which included guard Quinn Buckner and center Kent Benson in addition to May — was a wonderful group.

In 1978 Dutcher recruited one of the finest freshmen classes ever at Minnesota. The newcomers included a great pair of guards, Darryl Mitchell and Trent Tucker, center Gary Holmes, and a forward from Toronto, Leo Rautins, who had been named the high-school player of the year for all of Canada his senior season.

Combining with McHale, a junior by this time, the freshmen put a lot of life into the program. What I remember about the late 1970s, though, was that the Gophers could not beat Michigan State. The reason was simple: Magic Johnson. Magic played only two seasons in college, but his Spartans knocked off the Gophers all four times the teams met during those years. In a couple of those games, the Gophers had gone ahead. Then it seemed like Johnson decided that, "Hey, I'm not going to let them win," and, virtually single-handedly, led a resurgence.

Another great performer of that period was Mike McGee of Michigan, a remarkable baseline player. He was a deadly shooter from either corner, but I remember him more for his moves along the baseline as he'd drive to the basket. McGee went on to a good, but not great, career in the National Basketball Association. I still think of him as one of the best college players I ever watched.

Leo Rautins left the Gophers after only one year, transferring to Syracuse, but Minnesota still had a fine season in 1979–80. This was McHale's senior year and the first season for Randy Breuer, the seven-foot-two center from Lake City, Minnesota. The Gophers went 17–10, good enough for a berth in the National Invitational Tournament (NIT). They won their first three games, which advanced them to the Final Four at Madison Square Garden in New York.

They got by Big Ten rival Illinois by two points in the semi-final game to go up against Virginia for the championship. This became the matchup of the freshmen seven-footers: Breuer and the Cavaliers' Ralph Sampson. Sampson may have had the bigger press clippings coming into the game, but I've always felt that Randy held his own against Sampson. Nevertheless, Virginia, with a better team overall, defeated the Gophers, 58–55, in what was a very good final game.

The 1981–82 season was the senior year for the much-heralded freshman crop of 1978. Only three of those players—Gary Holmes, Darryl Mitchell, and Trent Tucker—were still on the team by this time, but they played key roles as the team fought for the Big Ten title. In the second-to-last game of the Big Ten season, on a Thursday night, the Gophers clinched a tie for first place. Two days later, on Saturday afternoon, they would play Ohio State. A win would mean an outright title. A loss would mean a first-place tie with the Buckeyes.

On the wall above the balcony seats at the west end of the basketball arena at Williams Arena are the words "Big Ten Champions" with the years that the team won the title painted underneath. In between these final two games, "1982" had been added. Before the game with Ohio State, I saw Darryl Mitchell on the court, pointing to the 1982 on the wall as if to say, "That's our title, and we're not going to share it with anybody." They didn't. The Gophers defeated Ohio State, 87–75. This may have been Randy Breuer's best game as a Gopher. He had 18 points in the first half and wound up with 32 for the game. In his final appearance at Williams Arena, Trent Tucker had 23 points. They were the only Gophers in double figures, but that was all they needed.

Minnesota went to the NCAA, and this time they won their first-round game, beating Tennessee-Chattanooga by a point, before being eliminated by Louisville.

In the early 1980s a long-time tradition at Williams Arena came to an end. For years, there had been a preliminary game, often featuring an outstanding pair of Minnesota high-school teams, prior to the Gophers game. One of the preliminaries provided the only time I ever saw a basketball game end in a tie. The two teams in the preliminary game were knotted up at the end of regulation. At that point, the Gophers and their opponents came out to start their scheduled warmups. There wasn't even time for a short overtime so, by mutual consent of the two high-school teams, the game was a tie.

It was about this time that the NCAA decided that allowing high schools to play preliminary games prior to a Gopher game could provide the University with an unfair recruiting edge; as a result, it ordered them stopped. I miss them, and I think others do, too.

In the mid-1980s came more turmoil. There was already a cloud hanging over the team for the first part of the 1985–86 season as one of the players, Mitch Lee, had been charged with the sexual assault of a female university student in one of the dormitories the previous winter. The trial was held in early 1986 and, on January 14, Lee was acquitted of the charges and promptly rejoined the team.

The Gophers went on to win their next three games, the third one coming in Wisconsin on Thursday night, January 23. I didn't see the Gophers after the game. I was staying in a different hotel from the team and took a separate flight back to the Twin Cities the next day. When I got home, I heard the news. The airplane the Gophers were on had been stopped by the police on the taxiway. The entire team was ordered off the plane. After they were back in the terminal, each player was led out to a car where there was an 18-year-old woman who claimed she had been raped by three of the Gophers in the team's hotel early that morning. Based on her identifications, Mitch Lee and teammate Kevin Smith were taken into custody. A third player, George Williams, was arrested later that evening.

Lee, Smith, and Williams were eventually acquitted, but the incident had an earthshaking effect on the basketball program. The following day, Saturday, University of Minnesota president Kenneth Keller announced he was forfeiting the Gopher's next game, scheduled for Sunday afternoon at Northwestern. Soon after Keller's announcement, Dutcher resigned as head coach. It was such a sad way for such a decent man to step down. I still see Jim frequently. He's a color commentator for the basketball games on television. He's a most honorable man and a good friend.

Jimmy Williams, who had been an assistant coach since the arrival of Bill Musselman, was named interim head coach and directed the Gophers for the final 11 games of the season.

Needless to say, the three players accused were off the team, leaving the basketball squad shorthanded. They did receive some help as a couple of Gopher football players, including quarterback Roselle Richardson, were recruited to fill the ranks. For the most part, though, the Gophers went with an "Iron Five," just as they had done 14 years earlier following the suspensions of Behagen and Taylor.

When they finally played again, on January 30, there were more than 13,000 fans on hand at Williams Arena to see them take on Ohio State. It was quite an emotional evening as the Gophers upset the Buckeyes, beating them 70–65. Kelvin Smith, Tim Hanson, John Shasky, Marc Wilson, and Ray Gaffney played nearly the entire game for Minnesota. Dave Holmgren, the only reserve used in the game, saw a minute-and-a-half of action. Otherwise, it was all "Iron Five."

Gaffney was a freshman that year. He was an excellent outside shooter, but my best memory of Ray came off the court a few years later, when we crossed paths in the airport. He had just gotten his diploma, was heading home with it, and he was so excited when he told me about getting his degree. I've never forgotten how good he felt about it and how good it made me feel. It was a wonderful reminder of what it's all about.

Soon after the 1985–86 season ended, the Gophers hired Clem Haskins as head coach and a new era began. Haskins had been a fine player at Western Kentucky University in the 1960s and was named All-American his senior year. He was the third player taken in the 1967 NBA draft and played nine years in the league, with the Chicago Bulls, Phoenix Suns, and Washington Bullets. He then went back to Western Kentucky where he served first as an assistant, then took over as head coach in 1980. Six years later, he came to Minnesota to rebuild a program that had been devastated by the events of January 1986. He did have a great young forward to build around, Willie Burton, recruited by Dutcher. I've always felt that Clem was the ideal coach for Burton; he certainly guided him well through Willie's four years with the Gophers.

It didn't take long for Haskins to put the Gopher basketball team back into national prominence. In his third season, the Gophers went 17–11 during the regular season. During the 1989 conference schedule, they were nearly unbeatable at home. The highlight of the season came when they defeated Illinois, which was ranked Number One in the country at the time.

Minnesota won its last three Big Ten games to receive a berth in the NCAA tournament. They traveled to Greensboro, North Carolina, and knocked off Kansas State and Siena to advance to the Sweet 16. The Gophers did it without Richard Coffey, their great rebounder and team leader, who had injured his knee late in the season, but Willie Burton really came through. He had 29 points and 13 rebounds against Kansas State even though he had to wear a facemask to protect a broken nose. Psychologically, the mask may have made him even better.

The Gophers' season finally ended with a loss to Duke. Burton had 26 points and Coffey came off the bench to play 11 minutes, but Duke—led by Danny Ferry and Christian Laettner—was too much for them, winning 87–70.

The 1989–90 season turned out to be even better. It was the senior year for Coffey and Burton and for center Jim Shikenjanski and guard Melvin Newbern. Kevin Lynch, a junior from Bloomington Jefferson High School, joined Newbern in the backcourt and rounded out the starting five.

The Gophers finished the regular season with a 20–8 record and made it back to the NCAA tournament. They almost got knocked off in the opening round. Actually, the Gophers were lucky to get past the University of Texas-El Paso, which had Marlon Maxey, a former Gopher (and later a member of the Minnesota Timberwolves), on the squad.

The Gophers shot only 33⅓ percent from the field. Turnovers made the difference—Minnesota had only 10 and El Paso had 23. That was enough to help the Gophers prevail in overtime, 64–61, in what really was a dreadful game.

Thereafter came a string of three games in which the Gophers played as well as a team can possibly play. I've always been thrilled by what the Gophers did in this tournament.

In their next game, they beat Northern Iowa, 81–78. Willie Burton—hitting on 13 of 17 shots from the floor—finished with 36 points. The Gophers were heading back to the Sweet 16.

The regional finals were held in the Louisiana Superdome in New Orleans, and Minnesota's next opponent was Syracuse University. The Orangemen were led by Derrick Coleman and Billy Owens, who both became first-round picks in the NBA draft. The Gophers were definite underdogs, but they came through with an 82–75 victory. The big reason for the win was the play of the guards, Lynch and Newbern. They not only played excellent defense, but shot 64 percent from the field between them. Newbern finished with 20 points and Lynch had 18. As a team, the Gophers shot 59 percent, with an incredible field-goal percentage of nearly 80-percent in the second half. When you shoot like that, you'll probably beat anybody. This night they did. It was a wonderful game.

If they could get by Georgia Tech in the Sunday game, they would be going to the NCAA Final Four for the first time in their history.

It was an outstanding game. Georgia Tech kept hitting field goals from three-point range. Dennis Scott had seven three-pointers and 40 points overall. Kenny Anderson, their great freshman guard, added 30 points. The Gophers hung in and refused to drop out of this one. Willie Burton had 35 points, and Shikenjanski had an outstanding game, scoring 19. Once again, Newbern and Lynch played well with 19 and 12 points, respectively, but the Gophers couldn't quite pull it off.

Trailing by two, they got the ball back after a missed free throw with just seconds remaining. They raced downcourt and Lynch, still on the move, threw up a desperation three-point attempt from the right corner. It missed its mark as the buzzer sounded and Georgia Tech had a 93–91 win.

We broke for a commercial immediately after the game. As I sat there, I felt so good—not disappointed—because I knew the Gophers had played as well as they could have played, and they had gotten this far with talent that really wasn't as good as most of the teams they had beaten. Even though they had lost, that Syracuse game was the best I had ever seen a Gopher team play, and it really was one of the great thrills of my life.

Coffey, Burton, Newbern, Shikenjanski moved on. A year later, Kevin Lynch also graduated. New players will always come along. They won't make us forget the players of previous years; they will add to our rich store of memories.

So it is with players like Randy Carter, Chad Kolander, Ernest Nzigamasabo, Townsend Orr, Dana Jackson, Jayson Walton, Arriel McDonald, Nate Tubbs, and Voshon Lenard. The 1993 Big Ten season was the first with Penn State in the conference. The schedule stayed at 18 games, but the addition of the Nittany Lions meant there would be two teams Minnesota would play only once instead of twice, Illinois and Ohio State.

The Gophers held on to beat Illinois in their final home game. They then went on the road and beat Penn State before losing at Ohio State in the conference finale. They thought their strong finish would be enough for a wild-card spot in the 64-team NCAA tournament. They even held a party to celebrate, only to have it turn into a wake when they were passed over by the NCAA selection committee. Deeply disappointed, they settled for a berth in the 32-team National Invitational Tournament. A year before, they had been eliminated in the NIT's first round by Washington State before a very small crowd in Pullman, Washington.

This time, the Gophers would be at home to open the

tournament, but home wouldn't be Williams Arena, which was undergoing a massive renovation that had begun immediately after the Illinois game. Instead they played in Target Center in downtown Minneapolis, the home of the Minnesota Timberwolves. Almost 12,000 fans showed up to see the Gophers eliminate Florida, 74–66.

The NIT committee was pleased enough with the turnout that it also scheduled the second round game for Target Center. This time, over 18,000 people roared, stomped, clapped and stood as the Gophers topped Oklahoma by a score of 86–72.

Normally, their next game would have been on the road, but the NIT, recognizing that the cash register was clanging louder with ticket sales here than anywhere else in the nation, told the Gophers to stay at home one more time.

This time "home" was the Met Center in Bloomington, home of the Minnesota North Stars (who were playing their final season here before moving to Dallas). There was tailgating by the fans in the parking lot before the game, and a standing-room only crowd of more than 15,000 watched the Gophers handle the University of Southern California, 76–58, and then take a victory lap afterward as a way of thanking the fans for their support. Over 45,500 had turned out for the three games in Minnesota. After the victory against the Trojans that sent the Gophers to New York for the Final Four, many of the fans stayed to join the band and cheerleaders in singing "Hail Minnesota." They were savoring the moment, not wanting to leave. It was beautiful. The Gophers performance in the NIT had brought out the most resounding basketball fan phenomenon I can remember.

Now it was on to Madison Square Garden. Many Minnesota fans made the trip, giving the Gophers a great feeling of support even though they were far from home.

On Monday night, the Gophers faced the Providence Friars, another team that felt snubbed by the NCAA selection committee. It was a tight game in the first half, and the teams went to the locker room tied, 35–35. Early in the second half, though, Providence started to pull away. They outscored the Gophers, 18–7, in the first six minutes of the half to open up a commanding lead. The gap might have been greater if not for Voshon Lenard. The Gophers' sophomore guard had a pair of three-pointers to account for 6 of the team's 7 points during that stretch. Then, after the Friars had opened up their 11-point lead, Voshon contributed 6 more points as part of a 9–0 Gopher run over a two-minute span that pulled Minnesota to within two points.

Throughout the rest of the game, Lenard continued to contribute timely baskets and clutch free throws. In the game, Voshon made 9 of 12 shots from the field (including four three-pointers) and was perfect in three attempts at the free-throw line. He finished with 25 points, helping the Gophers to a 76–70 win that advanced them to the NIT championship game.

Their opponents two nights later were the Georgetown Hoyas, coached by former U. S. Olympic coach John Thompson and led by a six-foot-ten freshman, Othella Harrington, at center. This game turned into a great defensive struggle. The Hoyas, with their trapping defense, helped force 19 Minnesota turnovers. The Gophers were also tough on defense as they pressured Georgetown into 16 turnovers of its own.

Once again, it was the backcourt of Lenard and McDonald that came through for the Gophers. Lenard scored 11 of his team's first 13 points in the game and ended up with 14 points in the first half. The Gophers held a 2-point lead at the intermission.

McDonald got the hot hand in the second half to help the Gophers establish a lead. With four-and-a-half minutes to play, McDonald picked up a loose ball that squirted away from a scramble among the other nine players. Five of them fell to the floor. Arriel gave a nod to the players lying in the lane as he wheeled to the basket for a lay-up to put Minnesota ahead, 62–51. It was bizarre, and I thought to myself, "Nothing can go wrong now."

As it turned out, those would be the last Gopher points of the evening. Like Providence two nights earlier, Minnesota held an 11-point lead. Like Providence, they watched it dwindle.

Fortunately, the difference was that the Gophers did not let it slip completely away, but they sure made it a nerve-wracking finish. Harrington had a chance to tie the game in the final minute, but made only one of two free throws. However, Georgetown got the ball back, still down by just a point. The Hoyas had three chances in the last ten seconds, but had one shot blocked by Randy Carter and another bounce off the rim. Their final chance came when they inbounded the ball with four-tenths of a second showing on the clock.

The in-bound lob toward Harrington never reached him. Voshon Lenard intercepted the pass to preserve the Gophers' 62–61 victory and its first-ever National Invitational Championship.

It was appropriate that Lenard ended up being the player with the ball at the end. His outstanding performance in the last two games earned him Most Valuable Player honors for the NIT Final Four. Voshon had been great throughout the tournament. He really came into his own in those five wins, getting better and better as the games went on. The NIT turned out to be a showpiece for him.

Nonetheless, it was a team effort and a performance I'll

never forget. I developed a bad cold in New York that sapped me of my strength, but the Gophers' performance gave me energy. I can't remember ever feeling so bad (physically) but so good (emotionally) as when I broadcast those two games in New York. It truly was a magnificent way to wrap up my 37th year of broadcasting Minnesota basketball.

What lies ahead for Gopher basketball? I don't know but I'm looking forward to being a part of it.

The Fading Dynasty

I got my chance to broadcast the games of the Minneapolis Lakers after I moved from KUOM to WLOL Radio in 1955. I switched stations because a program director position became available, but the move also afforded plenty of opportunities to continue sportscasting.

As I mentioned before, I still did the 1955 Gopher football season for KUOM, even though I was actually employed by WLOL. I had changed stations so close to the opening of the football season that I would have left KUOM in the lurch otherwise. WLOL had a fine sportscaster named Red Mottlow. He was the sports director and did most of the play-by-play on the station. In the summer of 1956, Red decided to take a job back in his hometown of Chicago. I took over his position and his duties. As a result, I was able to do the announcing for the Lakers during their final four seasons in Minnesota, from 1956 to 1960.

By the time I arrived on the scene, the team's glory years were behind them, but what years they were.

The rise of the Minneapolis Lakers was one of the great success stories in sports. They came into being in 1947 when a pair of Minneapolis businessmen—Ben Berger and Morris Chalfen—purchased the Detroit Gems of the National Basketball League and moved them to Minneapolis. They didn't bring any of the players with them. It was well they didn't; the Gems had finished the 1946–47 season with a horrible 4–40 record. Instead, the Lakers built from scratch. They hired John Kundla as coach and signed a few players who had been standouts at the University of Minnesota, Tony Jaros, Don "Swede" Carlson, and Don Smith.

Their best player when they started was a former All-American at Stanford University, Jim Pollard. Then, a couple of weeks into their first season, they picked up center George Mikan, the greatest player of his time, who led them to the National Basketball League title.

The Lakers switched leagues in 1948, jumping to the rival Basketball Association of America. They were the cream of this crop, too, winning the championship again.

In 1949, the BAA and NBL merged to form the National Basketball Association. The Lakers were now in a league with 17 teams, thanks to the merger, but they were even better equipped to deal with it because of a pair of players they drafted out of college. One was Slater "Dugie" Martin, an outstanding guard from Texas; the other was Vern Mikkelsen, who hailed from Askov, Minnesota and played his college ball at Hamline University in St. Paul. Mikkelsen was a center at Hamline. That spot on the Lakers, of course, was held down by Mikan, so Vern was moved to forward. He made the transition beautifully and helped the Lakers win another title.

In their first three years of existence, the Lakers had won three championships in three different leagues.

With Mikkelsen and Pollard flanking Mikan, the Lakers had the most dominant front line in the history of basketball. Mikan was the tallest of the three at six-ten, which means that the trio would hardly stand out, in height, on a basketball floor today. In their time, though, they were giants.

Even though I wasn't involved with the team as a broadcaster, I followed the Lakers closely as a fan.

The Lakers were dethroned in 1951 but came back to win another three consecutive league championships, giving them six in seven years.

George Mikan retired following the 1953–54 season, ending the Minneapolis reign on the basketball world. They were still a fine, if not championship team, without him. When Pollard also retired a year later, though, they fell to the ranks of mortals.

Even so, they still had some solid players when I began broadcasting their games in 1956. Part of the fun for me was that I now had the chance to describe the action of several former Gophers, who had finished their careers at the university before I started broadcasting Minnesota basketball.

Dick Garmaker and Chuck Mencel I mentioned before, since they played in that six-overtime game against Purdue. There was also Ed Kalafat and, finally, Whitey Skoog. As a Gopher in the late 1940s, Skoog was credited with introducing the jump shot to the Upper Midwest, and high-school players across the state started copying his style of shooting. Unfortunately, Whitey was nearing the end of his career when I started broadcasting the Lakers. Because of knee and back problems, he played in only 23 games in 1956–57, my first year with the team, and then announced his retirement. Still, it was very satisfying to watch him and the other ex-Gophers.

No matter what the sport, you get to know the players on a team best when you travel with them. As a result, I didn't get to know the Lakers very well since, except for the post-season playoffs, I recreated the action from the studio back in Minneapolis.

Even though I traveled very little with the Lakers, the one player I did get to know fairly well was Vern Mikkelsen. Our Danish backgrounds gave us something to talk about, as did his hometown of Askov, where I had spent summers at my grandmother's house as a youth. We've stayed in touch through the years. Not long ago, Vern and I co-chaired the regional fund-raising campaign for the Danish Immigrant Museum in Elk Horn, Iowa.

I got to know the Lakers' coach, John Kundla, much better later on when he became head coach of the Minnesota Gophers. A good coach. A good man.

The Lakers didn't have an outstanding season my first year with them. They finished the regular season with a 34–38 record, although, remarkably, this was good enough for a three-way tie in the four-team NBA Western Division. (All four Eastern Division teams finished with a better record than any of the Western Division teams.) The Lakers did beat the Fort Wayne Pistons in the opening round of the playoffs. They then lost in the division finals to the St. Louis Hawks, who went on to defeat the Boston Celtics for the NBA title.

Of greater concern than what the Lakers were doing on the court as the season neared an end was what was happening off the court. The team's owners, Ben Berger and Morris Chalfen, had sold the team to a pair of Missouri businessmen (one of whom was Marty Marion, the St. Louis Cardinals' former great shortstop), who planned to move the team to Kansas City.

Fortunately, the deal left an option for local interests to match the Missourians' offer. A civic drive began to purchase shares of the Lakers and, within ten days, the necessary funds were raised to keep the Lakers locally owned and in Minneapolis—for the time being.

The new ownership—at this time, more than 100 individuals and businesses could claim a piece of the Lakers—was headed by Bob Short, a well-known businessman and politician in Minneapolis. New owners weren't the only changes in the Lakers for the 1957–58 season. For the first time in their history, the Lakers had a coach other than John Kundla. John was offered his choice between continuing as coach or becoming general manager. Tired of the constant travel that was part of coaching, Kundla opted for the latter. His replacement as coach was the great Lakers legend, George Mikan.

Unfortunately, Mikan couldn't match the great success he had as a player in the role of coach. They lost their first seven games of the season and didn't improve much from there on. In January, with the Lakers having won only 9 of 39 games, Mikan was fired as coach and replaced by Kundla.

Even though they didn't win too often, they had some players who at least made the games interesting. One was rookie Hot Rod Hundley, a flashy ball handler whose style made him a crowd favorite. Hot Rod still broadcasts games in the NBA and is a very funny man. One of his favorite stories involves the time in the early 1960s that he and Elgin Baylor combined for 78 points in a game. Never mind that Baylor had 71 of them.

One game the Lakers did win this season was against the Harlem Globetrotters. The Lakers had first played the Globetrotters in an exhibition game in 1948 when there was much debate about which team was the greater in basketball. The Globetrotters won that first game, as well as another one against the Lakers the following year, but they never beat Minneapolis again. When the rivalry between the teams had started, the Globetrotters were one of the greatest teams in basketball, despite the fact that they spiced their play with crowd-pleasing antics even then. With the integration of the NBA, however, the Harlem Globetrotters no longer had a virtual monopoly on the best black players. They began relying more on their comedy routines and, to this day, the Globetrotters remain a great attraction. The fact that they lost to the Lakers, who were on their way to finishing with the worst record in the league, shows how far the Globetrotters had fallen from a competitive standpoint by 1958.

What finishing last in the 1957–58 season did give the Lakers was the first pick in the college draft. The best senior in the country that year was Archie Dees, the great center for the Indiana Hoosiers whom I had had the chance to watch play against the Gophers over the previous few years. (The thing I remember about Dees was his beautiful hook shot. Those were the days of hook shots, and they were spectacular.)

In addition to Dees, another player—a fourth-year junior named Elgin Baylor, from Seattle University—was also available for the draft. Short used his number-one pick to select Baylor, even though Elgin had announced that he planned to return to Seattle for his senior season.

Bob Short was desperate to get a player who could put some fans back into the seats. Fortunately, he was able to sign Baylor and, sure enough, fans turned out to see him.

Until Michael Jordan came along a quarter-century later, I always felt Baylor could make more body changes in mid-air than any player I had ever watched. Baylor was solid and strong and almost impossible to move once he had established his position near the basket.

With Baylor on the team, the Lakers' attendance in Minneapolis increased to an average of more than 4,100 per game, up more than 1,300 fans per game from the previous season. However, that season, the Lakers played fewer games than ever before in the Twin Cities. Hoping to lure larger crowds by playing in cities that usually didn't get to watch National Basketball Association games, Short moved many of the games scheduled for Minneapolis to neutral cities across the country, ranging from Charlotte, North Carolina to Portland, Oregon, as well as several other cities up and down the West Coast. A couple of the games on the coast drew well over 11,000 fans, a fact that was not lost on Short. Even though these were still "home" games for the Lakers, they were like road games to me in that I didn't travel with the team. Instead of being at the games, I was back in the studio, describing the action as I read it from a Western Union wire.

Whether live or via a Western Union report, I enjoyed broadcasting the Lakers that season. They were a greatly improved team with Elgin Baylor, and rose to a second-place finish in the Western Division, although it was still 16 games behind the defending league champion St. Louis Hawks.

In the playoffs, though, they shocked the Hawks, beating them in six games to advance to the NBA championship round. For a team that had posted the worst record in the league the year before, this was a remarkable achievement.

Unfortunately, they were no match in the final series against the Eastern Division champion Boston Celtics. Boston swept the Lakers in four games to win the NBA title, their first of eight straight.

The final game against the Celtics was also the last as Lakers for Vern Mikkelsen and John Kundla. Mikkelsen was retiring after ten seasons with the team. He was one of the game's greats and I think it's a shame that he's not in the Basketball Hall of Fame. The same could be said for John Kundla, who resigned at the end of the season to become coach of the Minnesota Gophers. Kundla led the Lakers to six league championships. As a coach, only Red Auerbach of the Boston Celtics has more.

Elgin Baylor's college coach, John Castellani, was hired

to succeed Kundla. In addition to the new coach, the Lakers had a new place to play for the 1959–60 season. Bob Short decided to make the Minneapolis Armory the team's regular home. To me, the Armory was just that: an armory. I never felt comfortable broadcasting a game there.

The Minneapolis Auditorium, a few blocks away from the Armory, had served as the primary arena for the Lakers since they moved to the area in 1947. It was a fine arena for basketball, but it wasn't always available, particularly during the playoffs in the spring. Other events such as the Sportsman's Show could bump the Lakers and force them to find a different place to play. Usually, their alternative was the Minneapolis Armory, but they sometimes switched cities and played at the St. Paul Auditorium. During the playoffs the previous season, they even ended up playing one game at tiny Norton Fieldhouse on the Hamline University campus in St. Paul. No other place was available.

The lack of a regular home didn't help in drawing fans. Vern Mikkelsen told me that Elgin Baylor had shown up late for one game at the Armory because he first went to the auditorium, thinking the game was to be played there. As Vern pointed out, "If the players couldn't even figure out where the games were, how could anyone expect the fans to?"

Short hoped that adding some seats and making some improvements to the Armory to make it the Lakers' regular court would solve the game of "musical courts." Ironically, early in the 1959 season, the Armory wasn't available and the Lakers found themselves back in the Minneapolis Auditorium. This game was memorable for a reason other than where it was played. Elgin Baylor went wild against the Boston Celtics at the Auditorium, scoring 64 points to set a new single-game NBA record.

Unfortunately, this was one of the Lakers' few wins during the first half of that season. In early January 1960, Castellani resigned as coach. Short promptly hired Jim Pollard to take over. Since retiring as a player, Pollard had gone on to coach at LaSalle University. Now he was back with the Lakers.

Pollard had always been enormously popular in Minneapolis, so popular that WLOL decided that I should be on hand for Pollard's first game as Laker coach, even though the game was on the road.

So, for the first time other than the playoffs, I traveled with the Lakers. Their opponent for this game was the Philadelphia Warriors, even though the game was played at Madison Square Garden in New York City. (It was part of an NBA doubleheader with the New York Knicks playing in the other game.)

It was my first time in Madison Square Garden. This was the "old" Garden, located about 20 blocks uptown from the current Madison Square Garden. My vantage point for this game was in a cage suspended from a balcony. It seemed strange sitting in this contraption—I almost felt like I was going to be dipped in oil—but it allowed for an excellent view of the action.

Even with the new coach, the Lakers lost to the Warriors as Philadelphia's sensational rookie, Wilt Chamberlain, scored 52 points. Although they lost, it was exhilarating to watch a player like Chamberlain, and I was happy to go on the road for at least one regular-season Lakers game.

As it turned out, I was happy I wasn't traveling with the Lakers less than two weeks later. The team left St. Louis after a game with the Hawks, heading back to the Twin Cities in their DC-3. Shortly after takeoff, the plane lost its electrical power and its compass. It drifted off course, and finally made a forced landing in a snow-covered cornfield in Iowa.

While that event was exciting and turned out well, I do not regret having missed it.

The 1959–60 season proved to be a rather disappointing one for the Lakers. After their improvement the previous year that ended with a trip to the NBA finals, they dropped to a 25–50 regular-season finish. Still, they made the playoffs and came within a game of making it back to the championship series. They knocked off the Detroit Pistons in the opening playoff round, then forced the St. Louis Hawks to a seventh game in the division finals.

The Hawks won that game, which turned out to be the final game in the history of the Minneapolis Lakers. Although it wasn't official at season's end, I think all of us who covered the sport felt that there would not be a Minneapolis Lakers team when the next season rolled around. One month later, Bob Short announced he was moving the team to Los Angeles. The championship tradition for the team has continued in California. The Lakers have won six more NBA titles since moving to Los Angeles. As a franchise, only the Boston Celtics have won more titles than the Lakers.

That Grand Old Game

"What's your favorite sport?" That's a question I'm asked often, and my answer invariably is, "The one I'm doing or the one that's coming up next." However, it is interesting to look at the three sports I've done the most: football, basketball, baseball. What makes each so intriguing?

Football. Three things stand out for me.

One: the shape of the ball. The punter can drop the ball just the way he wants it, get his foot into the ball just the way he wants it, and then, when the punt lands, it still may take a crazy hop sideways or back towards the punter. You've seen the ball squirt from one arm to another on a fumble. The ball is not round, and therein lies one of the marvelous imponderables of the game.

Two: the first down. You always have that immediate objective. You don't have to score. If you get the first down, you move *toward* that scoring objective. The third down is one of the most interesting situations in sports. Either a team will keep its drive going or be forced to give up the ball with a punt.

Three: football is dependent on 11 men working as one to make an offensive play or a defensive maneuver successful. Nowhere is the team aspect more evident.

Basketball. It has more faults as a game than any other sport I've done. The concept of working to have a man draw fouls so that he will *leave* the game or be less effective

145

in the game is a negative concept. The game is also determined too much by the quality of the officiating (and, believe me, with its tempo, the game is impossible to officiate anywhere near perfection). But when a basketball game gets into a rhythm, a reasonably uninterrupted rhythm, it has speed, style, and grace, along with considerable muscle.

Baseball. I enjoy *broadcasting* baseball. I sometimes become bored as a spectator. But it does have so many possible plays that can change the outcome of a game. There are the different ways of advancing a runner, by bunt, steal, slow grounder, or a long fly, to name just a few. There's the sudden home run that turns a game around, the 3–2 pitch with the runners on the move, the squeeze play, the swinging strike three. In the field, there's the third baseman cutting off the slow hopper toward shortstop, the outfielder racing—sometimes sliding—into the gap to snare a would-be extra-base hit, the catcher blocking the plate and taking the blow in a home-plate collision.

There are countless stories about Yogi Berra, the former New York Yankee great. The one I enjoy the most involves his style of hitting. The nicest way to describe it is that he was a bad-ball hitter; he'd swing at most anything, it seemed. Even so, he was an outstanding batter. So the Yankees, in their great wisdom, thought, "Well, if he's this good a hitter even when he's swinging at terrible pitches, just think how good he'll be if we teach him a few things." And that's what they did; they taught him to work the count, to be more selective as to what to swing at, and, basically, to think about what he was doing.

So what happened? Yogi's next time at the plate he looked at three called strikes. He stormed back to the dugout, threw down his bat, and growled, "How the hell can you hit when you're thinking?"

There's a lot of truth in that. A lot of the great hitters don't give much thought to what they're doing at the plate. They just know instinctively that, "Hey, this is where the pitch is coming. I know where there's a gap, and I'm going to hit it there." And they do.

Kirby Puckett would fall into this category. He's also notorious for swinging at bad pitches, but look at his results.

Of course, there is another side to this. One of the greatest hitters who ever lived, Ted Williams, was a real student of hitting. Williams' style is contrary to everything I said about Yogi. He knew what the count was and what kind of pitch to expect. To Ted, hitting was a science and that's how he dealt with it. Because of this understanding, Ted would have been a great catcher. He would have known exactly what type of pitch to call for in each situation. As it was, his knowledge of hitting helped him as a manager. When I started broadcasting the Twins, Williams was in his second season as manager of the Washington Senators. His biggest impact on the team was in their improvements as hitters. He took Eddie Brinkman—the classic example of a good field, no hit shortstop—and turned him into a pretty fair hitter.

I'm not sure if I could do a full season of any sport that had a schedule as long as baseball's for any sport other than baseball. Over a six-month period, a team plays in excess of 150 games. That doesn't leave too many days off. It can get to be a grind for anyone associated with the game: player, manager, broadcaster. However, baseball has a relaxed quality about it that's lacking in other sports, and baseball is a cerebral game. It keeps you thinking all the time. A team has a runner on first base. It can have the batter lay down a bunt to move the runner into scoring position, then hope for a single to bring him home, or it can hope for the dramatic "boom" of a home run that can turn a game around so quickly. It's the variety of the game, all the potential situations that exist, that make it stimulating.

I finally got my chance to do baseball play-by-play at WLOL, following Red Mottlow's departure. When Red left for Chicago in June of 1956, we were well into the baseball season. WLOL was carrying the St. Paul Saints at the time, and I immediately took over.

I remember that the Saints lost the first two games I did, and I got a couple of cards blaming me for the losses. "We were doing okay when Red was here," they said. The cards didn't bother me. I understand baseball fans and their superstitions.

I did the Saints for the remainder of the 1956 season and all of 1957. This meant I was there for the end of Lexington Park and the beginning of Midway Stadium, located just off Snelling Avenue a little south of the State Fairgrounds.

It was a thrill to broadcast from Lexington, where I had attended some games as a youth. I was only sorry that Nicollet Park in Minneapolis was gone by that time and I never had the chance to do any announcing from there.

I did the first broadcast ever in the Midway Stadium. Although the Saints were its original tenants, Midway Stadium was built with the hope of luring major-league baseball to it. The footings for the stadium were such that it could easily have been expanded into a much larger facility. It didn't happen, and I remember there were jokes that, with a zoo already in St. Paul, the city didn't need another white elephant. It was a very pleasant minor-league park. Midway Stadium was torn down a few years ago and replaced by a new stadium on the other side of Snelling Avenue.

The Saints had had some great years during their time in the American Association, but they couldn't get above fourth (out of eight teams) in either year I was with them.

Max Macon was the manager in those two seasons.

Roy Hartsfield, who became the first manager of the Toronto Blue Jays 20 years later, played second base for the Saints at the time. He was a good fielder and a team leader. I remember Roy telling me about an at-bat he had when John Mullen was umpiring. Mullen was one of the first umpires to wear glasses. In some ways, this might leave an umpire open to ridicule, but the players liked and respected Mullen. On this occasion, he called strike two on Hartsfield on a pitch that was clearly outside. Roy backed out of the batter's box and said, "Where was it, John?" Mullen replied, "It was outside, Roy. I missed it."

Hartsfield said to me, "What could you say to that? I just got back into the batter's box."

Another Saint I remember well was Stan Williams, who won 19 games for St. Paul in 1957. I got to broadcast games involving Stan when he came to the Minnesota Twins in a trade in 1970. By this time, he was a relief pitcher, and a good one, too.

I also remember John Glenn, a super young man. John always shined his shoes before every game. I asked him about that and he said, "Some day I'm going to get a break on that." Sure enough, it happened. There was a pitch low and inside. The umpire called, "Ball two." John said the pitch hit him in the foot and asked the umpire to look at the ball. When the umpire saw the shoe polish on the ball and the smudge on John's freshly shined shoe, what else could he do but award him first base. I almost expected John to look up at me in the broadcast booth with a look that would say, "I told you so."

Following the 1957 season, WLOL dropped the Saints games and picked up the Minneapolis Millers instead. As a result, I became the Millers' announcer. The Millers were playing in Metropolitan Stadium off the beltway in

Bloomington. The Met, like Midway Stadium, was built with the hope of it eventually being home for a major-league team. In Met Stadium's case, it was.

The situation for road games, whether it be for the Saints or the Millers, was the same as it was with the Lakers. I re-created them from a Western Union wire (all except for games in Minneapolis when I was doing the Saints or St. Paul when I was doing the Millers).

In 1958 when I took over broadcasting the games of the Minneapolis Millers, Gene Mauch, one of the most knowl-edgeable baseball people I've ever met, took over as man-ager of the Millers. The Millers were playing at Met Stadi-um in Bloomington at this time. Before the games at the Met, I liked to sit next to Mauch in the dugout, careful to keep my mouth shut and my ears open. I learned a lot about baseball by doing just that.

The only person, in my opinion, who could compare with Mauch as far as knowing baseball was Dick Siebert, the coach of the Minnesota Gophers' baseball team. I often sat and listened to Dick, but it was always in his office at Cooke Hall, not in the dugout.

I'd be at Cooke Hall, going to the basketball or football office, and Dick would stick his head out his door and say, "Come in here." He knew that I liked to talk and listen baseball, and both these things made him happy. I'd love to broadcast a Gopher baseball game sometime, but I never have.

Part of the fun of broadcasting minor-league games was the opportunity to watch players who went on to become great stars. I saw Harmon Killebrew hit a home run at Met Stadium several years before he became a member of the Twins. It was in 1958, when Harmon was playing third base for the Indianapolis Indians.

I also saw Ted Williams homer at the Met. Ted, of course,

had played with the Millers 20 years before. By this time he was a veteran with the Boston Red Sox, who were playing an exhibition game against the Millers at Met Stadium. Williams hit a prodigious blast over 400 feet for a home run in the first inning.

I remember that game for another reason. It was the first time I had been at Met Stadium when they had such a large crowd. I wasn't used to having so many cars in the parking lot, so I didn't make a mental note of where I had parked. After the game, I couldn't spot my car among all the others. I wandered around the lot, telling myself what a fool I was, until I finally found it.

The Millers were a farm team of the Boston Red Sox in the late 1950s. In 1958, they had players like Lu Clinton, Bill Monboquette, and Pumpsie Green, who later played with Boston. (In 1959 Green became the first black to play for the Red Sox, the last team in the major leagues to integrate.)

The Millers had a couple of good years under Mauch. In both 1958 and 1959, they won the American Association playoffs to go to the Junior World Series, in which they faced the champions of the International League.

The International League lived up to its name. The Millers opponent in the 1958 Junior World Series was the Montreal Royals. (The Millers swept the Royals in four games to win the minor-league championship.) The next year, they played the Havana Sugar Kings in the Junior Series.

Even during the playoffs, I didn't travel with the Millers, but stayed back in the Twin Cities to re-create the games from Western Union reports. When I heard how tense things were down in Cuba at the time (this was shortly after the revolution that brought Fidel Castro to power), I was just as happy that I didn't travel with the team.

Castro, a great baseball fan, was on hand for all of the

games played in Havana in the 1959 Junior World Series. I've been told that he wasn't above trying to intimidate the visiting players. Gene Mauch later said the Millers at times did wonder what would happen to them if they won. There was great concern for their personal safety. Castro's troopers were prominent in the stadium, lining the field and taking seats in the dugout. Mauch said that when Tom Umphlett, the Miller's center fielder, returned to the dugout after catching a Havana fly ball to end an inning, one of the troopers made a slicing motion across his throat. The message was evident.

Still, the Millers did their best to win. In the end, however, the Sugar Kings prevailed in seven games, winning the last one in the last of the ninth. The Millers were disappointed but at least happy to get out of the country safely.

I might add that the Western Union operator we used in Havana was very fluent in English. There was no problem "translating" his transmissions.

One of the players on the team at the time they played in Cuba was Carl Yastrzemski. Yaz had joined the Millers a couple of weeks before, while they were in the American Association playoffs. In fact, his debut created quite a stir.

In the opening round of the playoffs, the Millers played the Omaha Cardinals. The series was tied, two games each, and Game Five at Met Stadium was knotted up in the tenth inning. Mauch inserted Yaz as a pinch hitter to lead off the last of the tenth. He singled and later came around to score the winning run in the game.

Following the game, Omaha lodged a protest with the American Association, claiming that Yastrzemski was not yet eligible to play for the Millers. I believe this involved the player Yaz was replacing on the roster, who was leaving for military service. Omaha claimed that this player had not yet left and that the Millers shouldn't have been able to

Although I never broadcast from Nicollet Park, I spent a lot of time there as a youth, watching the Millers. *Star Tribune, Minneapolis-St. Paul*

It was great to be able to broadcast some Saints' games at Lexington Park in 1956, the last year for the stadium. *Minnesota Historical Society*

Gopher coach Dick Siebert was one of the
smartest baseball people I ever knew.
University of Minnesota

Gene Mauch, kneeling here at second base, was a player-
manager for the Millers in the late 1950s. He did so well he
got the job as manager of the Philadelphia Phillies in 1960.
Star Tribune, Minneapolis-St. Paul

I broadcast Twins' baseball from 1970 through 1973. *WCCO Radio*

Met Stadium was used by both the Twins and the Vikings. It was a great place to watch baseball but wasn't as good for football. A look at how far the seats are from the sidelines shows why. *Minnesota Vikings*

Bud Grant took over as Vikings' coach in 1967 and
took them to the Super Bowl in his third season.
Minnesota Vikings

Joe Kapp was the quarterback and inspirational leader of the
1969 NFL Champion Vikings. *Minnesota Vikings*

use Yastrzemski. The league upheld the Cardinals' protest and ordered the game replayed.

The teams then decided to play a doubleheader, with the replayed game proceeding the regularly scheduled game. The Millers won the replayed game to take a three-game-to-two lead in the series. If they could win the next game, they would take the series.

This game went 12 innings and the hero was Billy Muffett. He came into the game as a relief pitcher in the eighth inning and pitched scoreless ball, giving up only one hit in a little over four innings. Billy must have decided he had no desire to go back out to the mound again. As a batter, he led off the bottom of the 12th by hitting the first pitch over the right-field fence for a game-winning home run.

The Millers next played the Fort Worth Cats for the American Association championship. The Cats had Jerry Kindall, who had played on Dick Siebert's national championship team at the University of Minnesota in 1956. Kindall later served as an assistant coach with the Gophers under Siebert and then became head coach for the Arizona Wildcats, where he has won several national titles.

In this series, Kindall had three home runs for the Cats, but it wasn't enough. The Millers won the series in seven games for the right to play the Havana Sugar Kings.

Yastrzemski was finally declared eligible and played for the Millers against Fort Worth and against Havana. Yaz then spent the entire 1960 season with Minneapolis. He hit .339, second in the league, and was named the American Association Rookie of the Year. That earned him a promotion to the major leagues, where he succeeded Ted Williams in left field for the Red Sox. Williams, remember, had played for Minneapolis in 1938 before starting his great career with Boston. Now another Miller alumnus was taking his place. Like Williams, Yastrzemski ended up in the Hall of Fame.

I might add that, although he started his major-league career in the outfield, Yaz was a second baseman at the time he joined the Millers. (Prior to that, he had played shortstop at Notre Dame.) It always amazed me he could make the transition from infield to outfield so well. He was known for his great arm while he played left field for the Red Sox. Throwing from the outfield is far different from the throw you develop as an infielder. At shortstop or second base, you have to have a snap throw, but he proved he could uncoil from the outfield. Opposing runners were always reluctant to try to take an extra base against Yastrzemski's strong arm.

Yaz had a different manager to play for in his only full season with the Millers. Just before the 1960 season, Mauch was made manager of the Philadelphia Phillies. He had a fine career managing in the majors, with the Phillies, Montreal Expos, California Angels, and, of course, the Minnesota Twins. I've always felt bad that he never had the chance to manage in a World Series. He came close a few times, but something always happened to keep him from it.

Eddie Popowski managed the Millers in 1960. The team had a disappointing season, finishing fifth and missing the playoffs (the top four teams advanced to post-season play).

There was still great fan support for the Millers, but people in the Twin Cities at this time were getting the itch for major-league baseball. A few years earlier, a number of franchises began moving. We were seeing other Midwestern cities like Milwaukee and Kansas City getting teams, and we hoped we could become major league, too.

For a time, it looked like the New York Giants might move here for the 1958 season. At the last minute, though,

Giants' owner Horace Stoneham changed his mind and moved to San Francisco, joining the Dodgers, who were moving from Brooklyn to Los Angeles, thus placing two teams on the West Coast.

It seemed inevitable that the Twin Cities would get a major-league team of their own, either through expansion or relocation. (They were slated for a franchise in the proposed Continental League, a major league that never got off the ground.)

When the Millers finished the 1960 season, I wondered if this might be it for them. A few months before, I had broadcast the final game for the Minneapolis Lakers before they moved to Los Angeles. With the Millers, though, it wasn't as cut-and-dried that they wouldn't be back. Then, in October, Calvin Griffith announced he was moving the Washington Senators to Minnesota. Major-league baseball was coming to the Twin Cities. The Millers and Saints were history. Like other Minnesotans, I was thrilled that we were getting the Twins, but I was also sad. I would miss the rich minor-league tradition we had had in the area. I'd been a Millers' fan from as far back as I could remember, and your heroes as a boy always remain much taller than any heroes of today.

I also wondered if this would be the end for me as a baseball broadcaster. I wasn't sure if I'd ever do major-league baseball. Fortunately, ten years later I got the chance.

In 1970, the Twins needed another broadcaster to join Herb Carneal and Halsey Hall. Originally, WCCO couldn't decide between Al Shaver and me. Al and I divided the duties for the first few games. Finally, they decided to go with me. Had this been a competition for a hockey-announcing job, Al would have been far ahead of me. A native Canadian, Al's natural sport was hockey. He was the announcer for the North Stars all of their 26 years in Minnesota and I really don't think there has ever been a better hockey announcer anywhere than Al Shaver.

I was delighted to have the opportunity to do Twins' games, especially being teamed up with Herb and Halsey. What a pair they were. Halsey was such a character. He was well known for his love of green onions and cigars, a combination that could cause the person with whom he shared the booth a certain degree of discomfort. "Halsey enjoys a good cigar," Herb once said. "Unfortunately, those are not the kind that he smokes." At least when I was broadcasting, Halsey never started a fire in his jacket with the ashes from his cigar, something he had done in the past. Jerry Zimmerman, then a catcher with the Twins, remarked, "Halsey is the only man I know who can turn a jacket into a blazer in a matter of seconds."

And then there's Herb, the consummate professional. He started with the Twins in 1962 and is still as effective as ever. It was appropriate that he had the chance to broadcast their world championships in 1987 and 1991. I consider myself to be fairly knowledgeable about baseball, but I learned even more during the time I worked with Herb.

The Twins were enjoying the last of their early glory years when I joined them. They won the American League Western Division in 1969, but, despite that, Calvin Griffith decided not to re-hire Billy Martin as manager for 1970. Martin was always a controversial figure and ended up getting fired by several other teams even though he produced winning records in the ensuing years. History may have vindicated Calvin in his decision; even so, at the time, his firing of Martin was extremely unpopular with the Minnesota fans.

Bill Rigney, who had played with and managed the Minneapolis Millers in the 1950s, was the new manager in 1970. Under him, the Twins went on to another division title before losing to the Baltimore Orioles in the league playoffs.

In the four years I broadcast the Twins, they had some great players. The first one who comes to mind is Harmon Killebrew. Killebrew had won the American League Most Valuable Player Award in 1969. He followed that by hitting 40 home runs in 1971, the eighth time he had hit at least 40 in a season. That gave him 487 for his career, and we thought he would reach the 500 mark within the first two months of 1971.

It didn't work out that way. He got off to a slow start and was also hampered by injuries. The Twins decided to give out a mug commemorating his 500th home run. They scheduled the giveaway night for early July, certain that Harmon would have reached the milestone by then. July rolled around and Killebrew was still a couple home runs short. In fact, on the night they gave out the mugs, he was on the disabled list. It was another month before he connected with the big one. Against the Orioles on August 9, he hit his 500th, off Mike Cuellar at Met Stadium. Herb was announcing at the time, but I got to call number 501, which Killebrew hit later in the game. Despite the slow start, Harmon finished the season with 28 home runs and a league-leading 119 runs batted in. He went on to finish his career with 573 home runs, which was fourth on the all-time list at the time, behind Hank Aaron, Babe Ruth, and Willie Mays (Frank Robinson later passed Harmon).

Killebrew was a powerful man. The home runs he hit were mammoth. He was also a gentle man and a very nice one. I'd see him sign autographs for large groups of fans outside the stadium after a game, and he wouldn't shorten up his signature, writing H. Killebrew or scribbling his name illegibly. He made sure anyone receiving his autograph was getting it handsomely written.

Rod Carew was in his fourth year with the Twins when

I started. He was coming off an American League batting title in 1969 and looked like a cinch to win another in 1970. However, he was turning a double play against the Brewers in June when Mike Hegan made a hard take-out slide at second base (actually, it was more like a rolling block). Carew's knee was badly injured on the play and he missed most of the rest of the season. Rod missed out on a batting title as well but did win six more titles with the Twins. He finished his career with the California Angels and ended up with more than 3,000 hits and a spot in the Hall of Fame.

What bat control Rod had—a wonderful stroke, and he had amazing power for his size. He never went for the home run, but when he connected, the ball would take off and seem to be gaining strength as it left the ballpark. Still, he never hit many home runs because that wasn't his game. His style was to punch the ball through the infield or find a gap in the outfield. He could also lay down a bunt—he was one of the best bunters I've ever seen—and use his speed to beat it out.

Rod ran like a racehorse. He was so graceful he didn't seem to be running hard and sometimes fans felt he wasn't giving full effort. In reality, he was. Whether the effort showed or not, it was there.

Tony Oliva was another great player of that time. Oliva won the batting title his first two years in the league, in 1964 and 1965, and added another in 1971. As I watched him that season, I don't know if I had ever seen a better hitter. The ball really jumped off his bat. He hit to all fields and with good power. In June of 1971, Tony suffered a serious knee injury while making a catch in a game against Oakland. I had a sick feeling when he crumpled to the ground in right field. Often broadcasters' initial guesses about how serious an injury might be are very inaccurate. I wish mine had been, but I think all of us in the booth felt something very serious had happened that might have dire consequences. Unfortunately, we were right. Tony was never the same after that injury. He continued to play before having surgery for torn cartilage in his knee, and held on to win the batting title. More knee operations followed. He played only ten games in 1972 and probably would have been finished as a player had not the American League adopted the designated hitter rule in 1973. As a result, he was able to play several more years with the Twins. One of my great regrets in this life in sports is that Oliva could not stay healthy longer, because he would have been a cinch for the Hall of Fame.

Among the other Twins players who come to mind is Danny Thompson. Thompson first came up with the Twins to replace Carew when he was injured in 1970. He did a fine job playing all around the infield for the Twins over the next few years. Then, just prior to the 1973 season, we learned that Danny had leukemia. He was determined that the illness would not interfere with his play and, in that, he was an inspiration.

What a wonderful competitor he was. His teammates genuinely loved him. The outpouring of love that came with the knowledge of his leukemia was very real. Danny's will to win carried through in his reaction to the disease. He played with the Twins into the 1976 season, when he was traded to Texas. In December of that year, he died.

Bert Blyleven joined the Twins' pitching staff in 1970. He was only 19, the youngest player in the majors, but won ten games that year as a teenager. I'll never forget his first game, in Washington against the Senators on a Friday night in early June. The first batter he faced, leading off the last of the first, was Lee Maye. Blyleven came in with a three-and-two pitch and Maye hit it over the right-field fence, but that was the only run he gave up. He went seven innings before being taken out, and the Twins won the game for him, 2–1.

What I remember about Blyleven is that he often seemed to be cursed as far as non-support from his hitters went. The Twins rarely scored many runs for him. In 1971, he won three games by a score of 1–0. It's pretty tough when you have to be that good to get a win.

Blyleven had a great curve ball. The only other pitcher I recall with a curve that good was Camilo Pascual, who pitched for the Twins in their early years in Minnesota. Pascual, though, had more of a roundhouse curve. With Bert, the curveball was much sharper, tighter, faster. It really snapped off. I have often wondered what it would be like to stand up there and try to hit that curve. I admit I would not have had the courage to do it.

Bert left the Twins in 1976 (in the same trade that sent Danny Thompson to Texas), but later came back to Minnesota and pitched for the Twins in the 1987 World Series. It looked like he might have a third tour of duty with the team when he went to spring training with the Twins in 1993. It would have been nice if he could have made it, especially since he needed only a few more wins to reach 300. If he had made it to that level, he would be a shoo-in for the Hall of Fame. Although it's not a sure thing I think he still has a good chance to make the Hall. At any rate, I hope he winds up in Cooperstown.

When he first joined the Twins in 1970, Blyleven was already showing a couple of traits for which he became well known. One was his tongue, which he often stuck out of the corner of his mouth, especially when he wanted to get a little extra something on the pitch. He also had a very offbeat sense of humor. Over the years, he developed quite a reputation as a practical joker. He may hold the major-league record for giving the "hot foot" (inserting lighted matches in the shoes of teammates).

A couple of other characters I got to know with the Twins were Dave Boswell and Joe Lis. The word "flaky" is usually used in a kindly sense, and Dave Boswell fits that category. This Twins' pitcher was unpredictable, to say the least. He won 20 games in 1969, but is better remembered for a fight he had (and lost) with manager Billy Martin outside a bar in Detroit in August of that year.

I was told that, over the off season, Boswell was going stir-crazy around his home in Baltimore and wanted to get away, anywhere. Finally, he told his wife, "I'm going down to the bus depot and take the first bus out of town."

The next day, he called his wife. "I'm in Montreal, and I'm freezing to death!"

Her reply: "Couldn't you have waited for another bus?"

A couple of years later, the Twins traded for Joe Lis, a player who was anything but shy. Once, before a game at Municipal Stadium in Cleveland, the sky to the northwest suddenly changed colors, turning ominous shades of green and yellow and black. Then the skies opened up, producing a blinding rain that flooded the dugouts to the point of overflowing.

Undaunted, Lis took off his uniform and, clad only in long johns, swam the length of the dugout and back.

My first season with the Twins, in 1970, was the last for Bob Allison. I had admired Allison greatly as a fan in the 1960s. He and Killebrew gave the Twins a great one-two punch with their power. In the early years, Bob played right field for the Twins and had one of the best throwing arms in the league. Allison was also a great competitor, a real hard-nosed player. He didn't play much in 1970 and hit only one home run, but it was a big one, a two-run shot that tied a game against Detroit in the ninth inning in July.

The Twins didn't have much trouble that year in win-

ning their second-straight Western Division championship. Their main competition from the year before, the
Oakland A's, got off to a sluggish start and never gave
them much trouble. The team that did compete for much
of the season was the upstart California Angels. The Angels had finished 20 games under .500 in 1969, but they
stayed relatively close to the Twins for most of the 1970 season. In fact, they were only three games out of first when
they began a three-game series against the Twins in early
September. The Twins swept that series, effectively ending
the Angels' hopes.

Jim Perry was the pitching star for the Twins. He won 24
games and just missed number 25. He had a big lead
against Kansas City in his last start but was taken out in order to give him some rest for the upcoming playoffs. The
bullpen couldn't hold the lead, though, costing him a 25th
victory.

Jim was a very classy man. A couple of weeks before
that, he had a chance to pitch the division-clinching game
in Oakland. The Twins had champagne on ice in the club-
house in anticipation of the celebration that would follow,
but the night belonged to a young Oakland lefthander,
Vida Blue, who pitched a no-hitter against the Twins. After
the game, Perry sent one of the bottles of champagne to the
Oakland locker room for Blue.

One game that really stands out in my mind took place
in August, against Boston at Met Stadium. In the fourth inning, I saw the first-base umpire run in, calling time. I
didn't know the reason for it until Bob Casey, the Twins'
public-address announcer, announced that the Bloomington police had been informed that there would be an explosion at the stadium at 9:30, 15 minutes later. I'd seen many
games delayed by rain, but this was the first time I experienced one stopped by a bomb threat.

162

The Twins took no chances. Only a week before, a bomb actually had gone off at the Federal Building in downtown Minneapolis. They ordered the stands cleared. The players and other officials went out onto the field until further notice. The fans were supposed to go to the parking lot, but many of them joined the players and our broadcast crew on the field. What a carnival atmosphere it was out there, the fans mingling with the players, seemingly unconcerned that there might actually be an explosion. The beer vendors set up shop on the bases and quickly sold out. Other vendors walked among the crowd, hawking their wares just as if they were in the stands.

I felt inconvenienced by the delay, but not bothered or worried. I had been through a bomb threat a few years before, when I did a weather show for WCCO Radio from the top of the Foshay Tower, the tallest building in Minneapolis at the time.

When no bomb materialized, the Twins' management gave the all clear at 9:45, the field cleared, and the game resumed shortly after.

The Twins met the Baltimore Orioles in the playoffs, but the results once again were disappointing. For the second year in a row, Baltimore swept Minnesota in three games (the playoffs were best-of-five affairs originally).

The Twins lost the first two games, at Met Stadium, by scores of 10–6 and 11–3, but they were actually exciting games. In the first one, Baltimore knocked Perry out in the fourth inning with seven runs to take a 9–2 lead. The big blow was a grand slam by Orioles' pitcher Mike Cuellar on a fly ball that looked like it would be foul. In fact, it was well into foul territory when the wind blew it back. It landed just beyond Oliva's reach in the first row of the right-field seats, just inside the foul pole.

The Twins came back, helped by a tremendous home

run by Killebrew to straightaway center. In the seventh, the Twins were down by four but had a couple of runners on when Brant Alyea hit a long drive to center. The Orioles' great centerfielder, Paul Blair, made one of the best catches I've ever seen. Running straight back, he lunged for the ball and flicked it into the air with the heel of his glove, then maintained enough control to catch it before it hit the ground. That ended the Twins' last threat.

The next day, the Twins trailed by only a run when Baltimore exploded for another seven-run inning, this time in the ninth, to put that one out of reach. The following day in Baltimore, the Orioles won again to end the Twins' season.

Who was to know that it would be 17 years before the Twins would win another division title. They dropped to a 74–86 record in 1971, their worst since their first year in Minnesota. Perhaps, more significantly, for the first time since moving here, they failed to draw a million fans. In fact, they would have only two more seasons with attendance topping a million in the rest of their years at Met Stadium.

Oakland won the Western Division in 1971, helped in large part by Vida Blue, the young flamethrower who had no-hit the Twins the year before. This was Vida's first full year in the majors. He lost his first game of the season but then won 15 in a row before losing another. The way he was going I had the feeling he might win 30, but he tailed off, finishing the season with 24 victories. That was good enough to earn him both the Cy Young and Most Valuable Player awards. He was a gifted pitcher with a great arm, but he never came close to duplicating the magic he had in 1971.

This was also the last season for shortstop Leo Cardenas, who had played with the Twins since 1969. I had first seen

Leo in the games at Met Stadium in the 1959 Junior World Series when he played for the Havana Sugar Kings. Cardenas went on to a fine career with Cincinnati before being traded to the Twins. By this time, he had lost some of his range at shortstop but was still as surehanded as ever with the balls he could get to. He would gobble up grounders hit at him and make the play almost without fail. In 1971 he set an American League record and tied a major-league mark by making only 11 errors. Another fun player to watch at that time was Cesar Tovar. He could play anywhere and once did. In 1968, Cesar played all nine positions in one game for the Twins. He was a spark plug as the lead-off hitter, a pesky batter who could always find a way to get on base.

The Twins got off to a fast start in 1972, even though the start of the season itself was delayed ten days by a players' strike. When it did get going, the Twins won 16 of their first 21 games to take the lead in the Western Division.

Their hot streak was halted in a strange way. On a Friday night in the second week of May they played the Milwaukee Brewers in a game that eventually went 22 innings. This game was actually stopped by the American League's 1:00 A.M. curfew after 21 innings. It would be resumed the next day, preceding the regularly scheduled game.

As I drove home, I wondered how many more innings it would take to finish it. I knew the major-league record for the longest game was 26 innings. Wouldn't you know it, when the game resumed, the Brewers promptly scored a run in the top of the 22nd, then held on to win.

If that wasn't enough, the scheduled game that followed went 15 innings. I really hadn't gotten tired the night before during that marathon, but I started to wear down as they played another long one. The 37 innings for two-consecutive games set a major-league record that, I believe, still stands.

One of the reasons for the Twins' great start was a new outfielder, Bobby Darwin. He had six home runs through early May to lead the league. Then he started seeing curve balls, which proved to be his weakness. It reminded me of the saying that is supposed to have been uttered by many young phenoms: "I'm coming home, Ma. They're starting to throw curve balls."

Along with Darwin, the rest of the hitters dropped off in 1972. Even though the Minnesota pitchers posted an earned-run average of 2.84, a team record, the Twins finished with a 77–77 record for a third-place finish.

With the team slumping in July, Bill Rigney was fired as manager. He was replaced by Frank Quilici, who had been extremely popular with the fans during his days as a Twins player and was a coach on the team at the time he got the job.

Frank is a man you cannot help but like. I don't know if he was a good manager or not. Probably there were many other jobs he could have done a whole lot better. He's a great salesman, I know, and he's the type who can accomplish almost anything he sets out to do. As a manager, he was a lot of fun to be around.

The choice of Quilici as manager went over well with both the fans and the players. I know the Twins really wanted to win their first game for him. They played the Yankees at Met Stadium in his debut and trailed, 2–1, in the seventh inning when Killebrew hit a two-run homer to win it for him. Unfortunately, the wins didn't come all that frequently for Frank over the next few years. He lasted through the 1975 season before being fired.

The 1973 season was another lackluster year. Killebrew was hampered by injuries throughout the year and played in only 69 games, hitting just five home runs. There were a lot of new faces on the team in 1973. The newest belonged to Eddie Bane, a left-handed pitcher who came to the majors directly from Arizona State University. He had had a 15–1 record for Arizona State in 1973, including a win in the College World Series against the Minnesota Gophers.

Calvin Griffith hoped the young man could help put some fans in the stands, so instead of sending him to the minors initially for some seasoning, he put him on the major-league roster. The Twins announced that Bane would pitch on the Fourth of July, against Kansas City, and more than 45,000 fans turned out for his first game.

He had a herky-jerky motion, much like a left-handed Luis Tiant. As he wound up, he sometimes turned completely around, facing center field á la Tiant, before rotating back to deliver the pitch. He pitched well and received a standing ovation when he was taken out in the eighth inning. He didn't get the decision in the game, which the Twins eventually lost.

Bane finished the season with an 0–5 record, but his debut did provide a bright spot to an otherwise mostly dismal year.

The 1973 season would be my last as a baseball broadcaster. My contract to do Twins' games wasn't renewed for 1974. Some members of the organization felt I was too frank with some of my comments about the Twins' play that year. I've never seen myself as a negative broadcaster, but if the team wasn't playing well, I had to report it. Today the tendency among broadcasters is to "tell it like it is," but that wasn't all that popular back then.

Broadcasting baseball was fun while it lasted, and, who knows, maybe before I retire I'll have the chance to broadcast that Gopher baseball game that I've always wanted to do.

I described the action during Fran Tarkenton's first tour of duty
with the Vikings. *Minnesota Vikings*

The Purple Gang

I had my hands full in the 1960s, doing two Gopher sports along with my other duties in radio, but in 1966, another opportunity presented itself—one too good to pass up: the opportunity to broadcast Minnesota Vikings football on WCCO. I would also get to do the games with Paul Giel as my broadcast partner.

It was a good time to be announcing the Vikings on radio. Back then, home games were blacked out on television, whether the game was sold out or not. Some fans drove to Duluth or Rochester—far enough away that the games were televised—but, for the most part, WCCO Radio had a monopoly on the listeners for the team's home games at Met Stadium.

The Vikings joined the National Football League in 1961 as an expansion team. They performed as you would expect an expansion team to—not very well. They shocked the Chicago Bears in the first game of their first season, beating them, 37–13, but, for the most part, they lost a lot more often than they won.

They did provide fans with some entertaining moments, especially in 1964 when defensive end Jim Marshall scooped up a fumble against the San Francisco 49ers and ran 66 yards into the end zone. The only problem was, he ran the wrong way, into the wrong end zone.

Actually, they had a pretty good year in 1964, their first

winning season with a record of eight wins, five losses, and one tie, good for a second-place tie in the NFL's Western Division. The next year, though, they dropped back to a fifth place finish.

They were a colorful bunch, particularly their two leaders: coach Norm Van Brocklin and quarterback Fran Tarkenton.

Van Brocklin had gone from the playing field right into coaching in 1961. He had been a great quarterback himself for both the Los Angeles Rams and Philadelphia Eagles. In 1960 he had led the Eagles to the NFL championship. On the heels of that, he retired as a player and took over as coach of a brand-new team.

The "Dutchman," as Van Brocklin was called, was a difficult person to get to know. He was a genius in terms of offensive strategies, and certainly the right man for the Vikings in their early years, but he was not an easy man for a broadcaster to deal with. You never knew what kind of an answer you were going to get from him. Sometimes he could be very cordial; other times he snapped. I usually found myself going to one of his assistant coaches, all of whom were really nice people and most helpful. If I needed information, they had the answers.

On the other hand, I got to know Fran Tarkenton very well and always enjoyed my association with him. He was a charming man and a very funny one, too. I remember going to church with him once. Fran was a Protestant (the son of a preacher man, he was proud to say), but on this occasion he went to Mass with Grady Alderman, the Vikings' great offensive tackle, and me. This was back in the days when they rang the bell quite frequently at Mass and everybody genuflected. We were up and down for the whole Mass. As we were leaving the church, I heard Fran say to Grady, "Now I know why you have all that knee trouble."

Van Brocklin and Tarkenton were strong personalities, and there were often conflicts between them. Norm never really saw eye-to-eye with Tarkenton on how a quarterback should operate. Fran was a scrambler, thrilling fans as he eluded enemy tacklers with his quick feet. While his style was popular with the fans, it didn't sit well with the coach. Van Brocklin thought quarterbacks should stay in the pocket, as *he* had during *his* career. Of course, the Dutchman normally had a stronger offensive line in front of him to provide protection. Without that same advantage, Fran found his own way to survive. He scrambled. Even when defensive linemen got through the wall of Viking blockers, they found that their work was far from done. Breaching the offensive line was one thing; catching Tarkenton was another.

Early in the 1966 season, Tarkenton went on one of the greatest scrambles I have ever seen. In a game against the Dallas Cowboys in the Cotton Bowl, he dropped back for a pass and, unable to find a receiver, rolled to his right. He still couldn't find anyone open as he got close to the near sideline. With a few Dallas linemen about to converge on him, he took off to his left and crossed the field to the far sideline. Once more he set up, decided there was no one to pass to, and took off again for the near sideline, narrowly eluding a few more Cowboys. Back and forth he went, with the Dallas defense in futile pursuit, until he finally fired a pass to one of his running backs, Jim Lindsey. The gain was for barely more than ten yards, far less than the distance Tarkenton himself had run. Someone calculated that Tarkenton had scrambled back and forth for 23 seconds, an incredible amount of time, before getting off his pass. I can only imagine the things Van Brocklin must have been thinking during that play.

Despite Fran's heroics, the Vikings lost that game, as

well as many others that season. It was a disappointing year as the team finished with a 4-9-1 record.

At times, Van Brocklin was able to keep his sense of humor. In a November game at Met Stadium, the Vikings lost by a point to Detroit. The Lions' Hungarian placekicker, Garo Yepremian, kicked six field goals. Asked after the game how to stop Yepremian, the Dutchman replied, "Tighten the immigration laws."

He wasn't as jovial after a loss three weeks later to the Atlanta Falcons at Met Stadium. Neither was Fran Tarkenton. The Falcons were an expansion team in 1966 and should not have been a problem for the Vikings. Tarkenton was looking forward to the game for another reason. A native of Georgia, Tarkenton knew that many of his friends and family would be watching the game on television.

Fran didn't get to perform for his people back home. Van Brocklin chose to play Bob Berry at quarterback instead, and the Vikings lost, 20-13. Tarkenton was furious. The rift between the quarterback and coach was quickly becoming too large to heal.

Following the season, Tarkenton announced that he wanted to be traded. Soon after, Van Brocklin resigned as coach. I thought this might cause Fran to reconsider, but he remained adamant that he wanted to go elsewhere. Finally, the Vikings were able to make a deal with the New York Giants, receiving four high draft choices over the next three years for Tarkenton.

The loss of Tarkenton was a big one (of course, six years later he came back to Minnesota in another trade), but in retrospect, it was this trade that was the beginning of the Viking dynasty. The players the Vikings got with the draft picks from the Giants ended up being a couple of outstanding offensive linemen, Ron Yary and Ed White; Bob Grim, a wide receiver; and Clint Jones, a running back who had played on those great Michigan State teams.

The Vikings picked up two other stars in the 1967 draft: wide receiver Gene Washington, a teammate of Jones at Michigan State, and Alan Page, a defensive tackle from Notre Dame. Page became one of the best defensive linemen in the game. In 1971, he became the first defensive player in history to be named the league's Most Valuable Player. Today, Alan is both a member of the Football Hall of Fame and a Minnesota Supreme Court justice.

The Vikings still needed a coach and a quarterback for the upcoming 1967 season. They found people in Canada to fill both slots.

Just a few days after trading Tarkenton, the Vikings hired Bud Grant, who had coached the Winnipeg Blue Bombers to four Grey Cup championships in the Canadian Football League. Grant was well known in Minnesota. He was a native of Superior, Wisconsin, and a three-sport athlete at the University of Minnesota. He even played basketball over two seasons for the Minneapolis Lakers before switching sports to play football.

The Vikings filled the quarterback position with another man from the CFL, Joe Kapp, one of the most hard-nosed players I've ever watched. Grant apparently agreed with this assessment. He once said, "Other quarterbacks run out of bounds; Kapp turns upfield and looks for someone to run into." Grant and general manager Jim Finks (one of the best people I've ever worked with—he would have been the perfect NFL commissioner) got in touch with Kapp and made the deal.

I recall when Joe came to Minnesota right after signing a contract with the Vikings. I was on the air with "On the Go," my nighttime show at WCCO Radio, when a listener called to say that Kapp was in town. The caller even knew the motel in which Kapp was staying.

I thought, "What the heck, I'll try reaching him. I called the motel and asked, "Do you have a Joe Kapp registered there?" The operator said, "Yes, we do," and before I knew it, she had rung his room and I had Kapp on the phone.

I told him who I was and asked if we could do an interview on the air. He said, "Well, I've had a couple of drinks, so I can't promise you anything." I told him I would be careful, would respect his dignity, and would try to govern the interview accordingly. With that, he said, "Okay, let's give it a shot."

He was wonderful, no problem at all. He was relaxed, gave a good interview, and we were the first ones to get him on the air.

Joe was a competitive leader. I can't think of any other quarterback, ever, with his *fire!* Fran Tarkenton had a never-say-die attitude, but it was a different kind of spirit. So it was with almost any other quarterback you could name, but Kapp was a sort of street brawler. If that's what it took to win, that's how he would play it. His passes were terrible to look at — not the nice tight spirals you'd see from the classic quarterbacks — but it seemed they always got to the receiver when it counted the most.

Despite all the changes, the Vikings did not have a good season in 1967. They lost their first four games before beating the defending Super Bowl champion Green Bay Packers to give Bud Grant his first win as Viking coach.

The Vikings won only two other games that season, but one of them was over Fran Tarkenton and the New York Giants. Fran returned to Met Stadium and threw three touchdown passes, but the Vikings rallied from a 17-point deficit to win, 27–24, on a field goal by Fred Cox late in the game.

Even though it was a tough season for the team, there were some bright spots. They had a powerful pair of running backs in Dave Osborn and Bill "Boom Boom" Brown. Osborn finished the season with 972 yards rushing (a team record until Chuck Foreman broke it in 1975), second in the league to Cleveland's Leroy Kelly.

Coming out of the backfield, Osborn and Brown also proved to be among Kapp's favorite receivers during the year. Osborn led the team with 34 receptions, and Brown was third. (Sandwiched in between the pair was Paul Flatley, who later became my broadcast partner on Gopher football).

The Vikings finished at the bottom of the Central Division standings, but they were setting the stage for better things in 1968.

The Vikes won three of their first four games in the 1968 season and found themselves atop the Central Division standings. Never before had Minnesota been in first place this far into the season. Their one loss had been to Chicago. It was also the Bears' only win to date. As it turned out, the Vikings' greatest challenge to the Central Division title would be from the Bears, not from the Green Bay Packers, who were, once again, the defending Super Bowl champions.

After the fast start, the Vikings lost their next two games before getting a rematch against the Bears at Wrigley Field in Chicago. Trailing entering the fourth quarter, the Vikings took a 24–23 lead following a 26-yard touchdown pass from Kapp to Gene Washington with just over a minute left in the game. But the Bears came downfield and Mac Percival kicked a 47-yard field goal with three seconds to go to give Chicago a two-point win. This put the Bears and Vikings in a second-place tie in the Central Division.

Even though he didn't score a touchdown for the Bears, Gale Sayers rushed for 143 yards in the game. In the earlier game against Minnesota, Sayers also had more than 100 yards on the ground. He was one of the greatest running backs I had ever had the chance to watch. His long stride was classic.

The Vikings ended their three-game losing streak with a 27–14 win over Washington in a game that featured a 98-yard punt return for a touchdown by Charlie West. It came following a 60-yard punt by the Redskins' Mike Bragg. West had to go back for the punt and didn't realize how close he was to his own goal line. I wondered why he didn't let the ball go into the end zone for a touchback, but since Bragg had outkicked his coverage, West had plenty of running room as he started back upfield. He broke through the Washington defenders with only Bragg left to stop him. Bragg was blocked out, though, by Jim Marshall and Earsall Mackbee and West went into the end zone with a runback of 98 yards, tying an NFL record. The win put the Vikings back in first place along with the Bears, who won on a last-second field goal by Percival.

Both teams won again the following week. The Vikings beat Green Bay at Met Stadium. It was the first time Minnesota had ever beaten the Packers at home, and the first time they had won both their games against the Packers in a season. The Bears kept pace with the Vikings by topping San Francisco. It was a costly win, however. In the second quarter, Gale Sayers had ligaments torn in his knee as he was being tackled. He would be out the rest of the season. It was a tremendous blow to the Bears. On top of that, the following week they lost their fine young quarterback, Virgil Carter, with a broken ankle. The Vikings took over sole possession of first place. I wondered how serious a challenge the Bears could continue to mount without Sayers and Carter.

You really had to give the Bears credit, however. They stayed tough over the rest of the season. They seemed determined to win the title for Sayers and went into the final week of the season tied with the Vikings.

The advantage was with the Bears. If the teams finished the year tied, Chicago would advance to the playoffs by virtue of the two victories over Minnesota. The Vikings would have to defeat the Eagles in Philadelphia and have Green Bay win in Chicago.

Because we were in the Eastern time zone, the Vikings game began an hour earlier than the Bears game. It was a cold windy day at Franklin Field on the University of Pennsylvania campus as the Vikings defeated Philadelphia, 24–17.

Now all we could do was wait for the outcome of the Chicago-Green Bay game. Earlier, we had good news. Green Bay had opened up a 28–10 lead early in the second half. Chicago came back with two touchdowns and a field goal in the fourth quarter to cut the lead to one. The Vikings sat quietly in their locker room, pulling for the Packers to hang on. Sid Hartman managed to get the Packer-Bear broadcast from WCCO on the telephone and provided us with a running commentary of the game.

Late in the game, Chicago got the ball back near midfield following a punt. The last thing any of us wanted was for Mac Percival to get a chance to win the game with a field goal. Percival led the league in field goals that season, and the Bears were now within a first down of putting him into position for another one. (Remember, at this time the goal posts were on the goal line, not ten yards behind it as they are now.) Finally, Sid called out the news we had been hoping for. Ray Nitschke, the Packers' great linebacker, had intercepted a pass. The Bears' last hope had been blunted and the Vikings were Central Division champions.

Unfortunately, in the first round of the playoffs, the Vikings were no match for the Coastal Division champions, the Baltimore Colts. The Colts had lost only once all season and rolled to a rather easy 24–14 win over Minnesota.

The Vikings' season still wasn't over. Two weeks later, they went to the Orange Bowl in Miami to play the Dallas Cowboys in what was called the Playoff Bowl, which featured the runner-up teams in each conference. Minnesota got off to a 13–0 lead, but ended up losing, 17–13. Barely 20,000 people showed up for the game, and I can't say that either team seemed all that interested in the game. The Playoff Bowl lasted only one more year after this.

Although it ended with a pair of post-season losses, the 1968 season was certainly a memorable one, but even though the Vikings won a division title, there was no way it could prepare us for what was to come in 1969.

This became known as the Vikings' "40-for-60" season, referring to 40 men (the roster size at the time) for 60 minutes. In fact, at the end of the 1969 season, when Kapp was named the team's Most Valuable Player, he refused to accept the award. "There is no Most Valuable Viking. There are 40 Most Valuable Vikings," he said. That philosophy was fitting for Kapp and really did exemplify the Vikings' teamwork in 1969.

Actually, Joe was not even the team's starting quarterback at the beginning of the year. He didn't play in the season opener in New York against the Giants. Gary Cuozzo quarterbacked the Vikings and led them to a 17–3 halftime lead. The Vikings could manage only two Fred Cox field goals in the second half, but it looked like it would be enough. That is, it looked that way until Fran Tarkenton connected for two touchdown passes in the final five minutes to lead the Giants to a one-point win over his old team.

It hurt to lose that game, one the Vikes should have won, because their next opponent was the Baltimore Colts. The

Colts had lost only one regular-season game the year before and went to the Super Bowl before losing to the New
York Jets. In 1968, they had had little trouble in beating the
Vikings twice—once in the playoffs—and now were favorites to win again.

However, Joe Kapp was at quarterback for the Vikings in
this game and put on an unforgettable show. He threw six
touchdown passes in the first three quarters and had more
than 400 yards passing before he went to the sidelines with
an injured left wrist. Cuozzo took his place and it appeared
he would play the rest of the game since the Vikings had
a commanding lead. Then Bud Grant learned that Kapp
was within a few yards of the Vikings' record for passing
yardage in a game. Kapp returned to the lineup (with a broken wrist, as it turned out). He not only eclipsed the team
passing mark but threw another touchdown pass to give
him seven in the game, tying an NFL record held by three
other quarterbacks. One of those quarterbacks, Adrian
Burk, was a back judge in this game. He had a good view
of watching his record being tied.

The next week the Vikings played the Green Bay Packers
at Memorial Stadium on the University of Minnesota campus. The Minnesota Twins were in the American League
championship playoffs against the Baltimore Orioles and
had a game scheduled at home the next day. Rather than
have the field at Met Stadium torn up by football, the game
was moved to the Gophers' stadium. I felt right at home
from my spot in the radio booth atop Memorial Stadium as
I watched an awesome defensive display by the Vikings.
Eight times they sacked Packer quarterback Bart Starr, and
they came within five seconds of pulling off the first
shutout in their history.

That shutout came the following week, as they blanked
the Chicago Bears, 31–0, at Wrigley Field. The play that

stands out in my mind from this game involved Fred Cox; it shows how the ball can bounce when things are going right for a team. Leading 7–0, the Vikings lined up for a 47-yard field goal try by Cox. The attempt was blocked by the Bears, but the ball bounced right back to Cox. He tucked the ball under his arm and took off around the left side, finally ending up with an 11-yard gain and a first down. This kept the drive alive, and the Vikings went in for a touchdown.

Despite this strange play involving Cox, the day belonged to the defense. The "Purple Gang," as they called themselves, were led by Carl Eller, Alan Page, Gary Larsen, and Jim Marshall, who were being recognized as the best front four in the game. All four played in the Pro Bowl following the season. They were backed up by linebackers Wally Hilgenberg, Roy Winston, and Lonnie Warwick and a deep secondary that included Dale Hackbart, Karl Kassulke, Earsall Mackbee, Ed Sharockman, Paul Krause, and Bobby Bryant. I think sometimes that people focused too much on the front line, and, as a result, forgot how good the linebackers and secondary were. For example, they often said Sharockman was too slow to play at defensive back, but Ed was tough. He could play with any type of injury.

The Vikings' defense gave up only 143 points during the year, a record for the fewest points allowed in a 14-game season.

Minnesota easily won its next two games and then had a rematch with the Bears at Met Stadium. This time they won, 31–14, with Clint Jones capping the Minnesota scoring with an 80-yard touchdown run, a team record. The loss put the Bears at 0–7. They would go on to win only one game in 1969 after having been the Vikings' chief nemesis the previous year. I must admit it was nice to see Gale Sayers have a good game for the Bears. He was making a strong comeback from his knee surgery in 1968 and ran for over 100 yards, including a touchdown. The other Chicago touchdown was scored by Brian Piccolo. No one knew it, but Piccolo would play only two more games for the Bears. A few weeks later, he was diagnosed with leukemia. He died the following June. The movie *Brian's Song* is about Piccolo and about his close friendship with Sayers.

The Vikings next game, against the Cleveland Browns, was shaping up to be a classic. Both teams had only one loss, and the Browns had just beaten their Eastern Conference rival, the Dallas Cowboys, by a score of 42–10. It turned out to be anything but a close game. The Vikings scored the first nine times they had the ball and won by a score of 51–3.

Earlier, I talked about the good bounces that can come to a team. This happened again two weeks later during a 52–14 win over the Pittsburgh Steelers. The Steelers had just scored their second touchdown to put them within ten points. On the kickoff that followed, Charlie West ran the ball back for Minnesota, was hit at the 35-yard line, and fumbled. The ball squirted into the air, right into the arms of the Vikings' John Beasley at the 40. Beasley took off down the sideline, running 60 yards for a touchdown.

The Vikings were now 9–1 and could clinch the Central Division title in a Thanksgiving game against the Lions in Detroit. This was before the Pontiac Silverdome was built, although they sure could have used it for this game. The teams played in the snow and mud at Tiger Stadium, and by the second half, it was hard to identify the players because the mud was obliterating their numbers. As a result, there was a bit of confusion as to who was involved in a memorable play in the third quarter. As it turned out, it was Alan Page who rushed in and tipped Detroit quarterback Greg Landry's screen pass. Jim Marshall intercepted and, along with Page, headed toward the end zone. (Fortunately, this time it was the correct end zone.) As Marshall was grabbed from behind and was being taken down, he flung the ball backwards to Page, who ran it the final 15 yards for a touchdown. I think I was the only one of the broadcasters covering the game who knew it was Page who scored. Actually, I was guessing, because I couldn't read his number any better than the others, but I thought he ran like Page, so I went ahead and said it was Page. As it turned out, I was right. The Viking defense not only contributed directly to the scoring—as it had many times during the season—but it posted its second shutout. Minnesota won, 27–0, and clinched its second-straight title.

Their next opponent was also the team they knew they would be meeting in the playoffs. The Los Angeles Rams were 10–0, the last undefeated team in the NFL, and had wrapped up the Coastal Division title. I saw this game as being a key to how good the Vikings were. They had been soundly trounced by the Rams each of the last two seasons. Had they progressed far enough to beat them? Los Angeles had an excellent quarterback in Roman Gabriel; in addition, they were playing at home, in sunny southern California.

None of this seemed to bother the Vikings. Charlie West returned the opening kickoff of the game 78 yards, nearly breaking it for a touchdown. A few plays later, Dave Osborn crashed into the end zone to put the Vikings ahead, 7–0. They added another touchdown in the second quarter for a 14–0 lead. This drive featured a play that was classic Joe Kapp. He was running for a first down when the Rams' Richie Petitbon put his head down and prepared to tackle Kapp. Joe hurdled right over Petitbon, looking like a track star, and went on to an 18-yard gain. The Vikings had a

17–3 halftime lead, then held on for a 20–13 win, handing the Rams their first loss of the season.

Kapp's hurdle of Petitbon typified the kind of quarterback and leader that he was. Somehow, he always found a way to get the job done. Roman Gabriel was the league's glamor quarterback in 1969, but it was hard to beat Joe Kapp's performance.

The Vikings split their final two games of the season to finish the regular season with a 12–2 record, best in the National Football League. Now they prepared to play the Los Angeles Rams again. This game would be in Minnesota, in weather more to the Vikings' liking.

Even though they made no secret about their distaste for the sub-freezing temperatures, the Rams dominated the first half in this game and opened up a 17–7 lead. Things didn't look good for Minnesota, and it appeared this would be a sad ending to what had been a great season.

The fans, however, apparently wanted to convey a message to the Vikings as they came out of the locker room for the second half. The ovation they gave the team sent chills down my spine. There have been just a few, really a handful of instances in my memory, in which the fan reaction has been way beyond what you would expect. This was one of those times. It was almost supernatural — and I use that word advisedly. It's that type of ovation that sticks in your mind perhaps more than the game itself.

The tremendous fan support fired up the Vikings. They got a touchdown from Dave Osborn to cut the Rams' lead to 17–14. Los Angeles went up by six points on a field goal in the fourth quarter. The Vikings came back with a 70-yard drive that put them near the Rams' goal line with eight minutes to play. Kapp then took off on a bootleg around left end. He turned the corner and made it into the end zone untouched to tie the game. Fred Cox kicked the extra point, and the Vikings had a 21–20 lead.

Now that they had the lead, there was no way they were going to let it get away. Cox boomed the kickoff into the end zone. Ron Smith of the Rams decided to run it out, but he was crushed by Dale Hackbart on the 12-yard line. On the next play, Eller broke through the line, grabbed Gabriel in the end zone, and hurled him to the ground for a safety and a 23–20 lead. The fans went berserk, and I almost joined them.

Los Angeles did have another chance in the closing minutes. They were nearing midfield, hoping to get into position for a field goal that could send the game into sudden-death overtime. Then Gabriel threw a pass that hit Alan Page in the facemask. The ball bounced into the air, and Page grabbed it for an interception to end the Rams threat. The Vikings had won, and I felt limp. It was one of the most exciting games I had ever broadcast.

The win put the Vikings into the NFL Title Game against the Cleveland Browns. (This was the last year before the merger of the National and American Football Leagues, meaning that this would be the last NFL Title Game ever played.)

The game was played on another cold day at Met Stadium. After the exciting game against the Rams, this one seemed almost anti-climactic. The Vikings didn't romp as they had in their earlier meeting with Cleveland, but they had no trouble in winning, 27–7.

The play that stands out in this game involved, who else, but Joe Kapp. Kapp was running with the ball after being unable to find a receiver. He collided head-on with linebacker Jim Houston and flipped over him, hitting the frozen turf hard. Kapp got up slowly and at first I was afraid he was hurt. As it turned out, it was Houston who got the worst of it. He crumpled to the ground and didn't get up.

It didn't matter to Kapp how big the opposition was. He never turned away.

After the win over the Browns, a Super Bowl championship seemed to be a foregone conclusion. The year before, the New York Jets had upset the Baltimore Colts to give the American Football League its first win in the Super Bowl. No one expected such an event to happen again, but as we know now, lightning did strike twice.

The Super Bowl back at that time did not have all the hype or the ballyhoo that we associate with it now. It was played only a week after the league championships, not like the two-week gap there is today. I got to New Orleans the day before the Super Bowl. I recall that the Vikings were at a very even keel, typical of what you'd expect from a Bud Grant team. There were no pep talks for this game. Maybe that hurt them, it's hard to say, but in the long run, that stable form of leadership led to many great years following this one.

The Vikings were 13-point favorites to beat the Kansas City Chiefs in the Super Bowl. Instead, it turned into a very dismal rainy afternoon in Tulane Stadium. The Chiefs really controlled the game and played very well. We didn't. Kansas City won the game, 23–7.

I didn't know it, but this was to be my last game as the Vikings' announcer. KSTP Radio got the contract for the Viking games the following year. I would have liked to finish on a happier note, but I felt terrific about having been a part of the Vikings' rise to glory.

Even though I haven't been behind the mike, I have watched — and agonized over — the Vikings in three more Super Bowl appearances, all losses. I still hope that someday I'll watch them win one.

"You must be the nice folks who wanted to tour our studio."

This Richard Guindon cartoon from the 1970s indicates the "family" type of relationship WCCO has with its listeners. *Reprinted with the permission of the Star Tribune, Minneapolis-St. Paul.*

The Good Neighbor:
My Life at WCCO

In the summer of 1963, I was completing my eighth year at WLOL. Certainly I was happy there. I enjoyed my on-air duties and especially all the sports I was doing. Then one day, Charlie Boone of WCCO Radio's "Boone & Erickson" show stopped by WLOL to have lunch with one of the other announcers. I had never met Charlie before, but we had a chance to talk briefly. It was a chat that changed my life.

Charlie told me there was going to be an opening at his station; Bob Montgomery (who went by Bob White on the air) was leaving. "If you're interested in working at WCCO," Charlie told me, "you really ought to let them know."

"You know, I think I will," I told him, and I did.

First I talked to WCCO's program director, Val Linder, then their sales manager, Phil Lewis. After cutting an audition tape for them, I finally met with the station manager, Larry Haeg, Sr. When the interview was done, I had the job.

Initially, my main assignment at WCCO was hosting a program called "On the Go," which ran from 7:00 to 9:00 in the evening. We'd have music and guests, a little of everything. I did some newscasts following the show and went home at 1:05 in the morning. They weren't ideal hours, but that's to be expected in the radio business. From the beginning, I also broadcast the high-school football game of the week.

Beyond this weekly high-school game I wasn't sure what my opportunities for sportscasting would be. As it turned out, they would be many. I didn't know that at the time I took the job, but I was eager to make the move to WCCO just the same.

WCCO was then, as it is now, special. It has had a hold on its market like no other station in the history of radio. For a time in the 1960s and 1970s, its share of the radio listening audience in the Twin Cities was nearly 50 percent. That is unbelievable. That figure has shrunk, particularly with the growth of FM radio and the many popular stations on that band now, but WCCO is still one of the most dominant stations in the country. It is heard by people around the world. For many of these people, trying to pick up radio signals from faraway stations is a hobby. When I started working at WCCO, there was a map of North America on the studio wall. Judy Lebedoff and others from our promotion department would sort through mail from our listeners and put tacks in the map to indicate where WCCO had been picked up. I've seen the cards that have come in. To authenticate the fact that they really heard us, the listeners have to note things such as the time and date and information about the program that was on at the time, things that they would have no way of knowing if they hadn't actually picked up our signal. We stamp the card to verify it, and return it to them. Not only has WCCO been picked up throughout the United States, including Alaska and Hawaii, but we've received cards from as far away as the upper reaches of Norway and, on more than one occasion, New Zealand. A radio signal can travel across the ground or through the air. The airwaves reflect off the ionosphere in the atmosphere and come back to earth. After the sun goes down, layers of the ionosphere rise; this means that radio waves bouncing off the ionosphere can sometimes be picked up by people thousands of miles from where the signal was transmitted.

WCCO is a clear-channel station. Unlike other stations that either have to reduce power or restrict the direction of their signal at night to avoid colliding with signals from other radio stations on the same frequency, WCCO can boom its 50,000 watts in all directions, day or night.

This clear-signal capability made it possible for us to include people from far away in some of our programs, such as "Honest to Goodness," a telephone quiz show. Steve Edstrom and I hosted "Honest to Goodness" in the 1970s. People sent in cards with their names and phone numbers. We'd pick a card, call the person, and ask the question. The pot started out with $8.30 (for 830, our position on the AM dial), and if the person we called didn't know the answer, we'd add $8.30 to the kitty. On "Clear-Channel Night," we would pick only cards that had come from far away. We received cards from all over, but quite a few from the Ohio River Valley, where, apparently, our signal is very strong.

In fact, that reminds me of an incident after a Gopher basketball game against Butler University in Indianapolis. I took a cab back to the hotel, and when the driver asked what I did, I told him I had just broadcast the game. He asked my name and, after I told him, he said, "You do "Honest to Goodness," don't you?" I was amazed that he knew, but was amazed even more when he punched a button on his radio and I heard my voice. The Gopher broadcast was on a tape delay that night and there I was, announcing the game, with it coming over the WCCO signal as clear as could be, even though we were more than 500 miles from home.

WCCO has also been recognized many times for its outstanding programming. Many times it has received the highest honor in broadcasting—the George Foster Peabody Award for outstanding local public service. The walls in the conference room at WCCO are covered with Peabody Awards.

One of those I remember particularly well, because it involved E. W. Ziebarth, who was a commentator at the station when I started there. In the early 1970s, "Easy" had a heart attack. Centered around his personal experiences, WCCO did a special program about heart surgery titled "The Heart of the Matter." In addition to a Peabody, this show, which I was privileged to narrate, won awards from the American Medical Association, the American Heart Association, the Northwest Broadcast News Association, and others.

What makes WCCO special goes far beyond its market share, the power of its signal, or even its programming. More than anything, it is the feeling of "family" that extends to everyone involved with the station. This includes not only on-the-air personalities, but also reporters, producers, sales executives, switchboard people, and all those behind the scenes. To this day, I savor the daily contact I have with people in our organization—the conversations in the news room, the studios, offices, and hallways, as well as away from the station.

Equally important and integral parts of this family are the listeners. Those people who tune in every day really care about us and what is going on in our lives, both at work and away from WCCO. They send us cards on our birthdays and they call to find out how we're doing if we're sick. They share in the good things in our lives and commiserate with us if something bad happens.

Here's an example of this feeling of family. One Thanksgiving I was doing "On the Go" in the evening. Earlier that

day, I'd had a very nice Thanksgiving dinner that had included pumpkin bread made by my mother-in-law. On the
air, I was detailing my day a little bit, as you could do with
our audience, and happened to mention the bread. I didn't
think much of it, until we started getting cards and phone
calls from listeners, asking for the recipe. As a result, I
decided to make the recipe available to anyone who wanted it. Even though I mentioned it only once more after that
initial story, the station received over 200 cards and letters
asking for the pumpkin bread recipe.

I especially appreciate the opportunities I've had to get
to know our listeners in person, often through our travels
together. One of the marvelous bonuses of working at
WCCO Radio has come through the opportunity to host
some of the station's "Good Neighbor" tours to many
different parts of the world. Of the 25 trips Ramona and I
have shared, a majority have been under the "Good Neighbor" label. Journeying around the world with the people
on the tours has given me a chance to know our listeners
in a way few other announcers do. Perhaps it was prophet-
ic that my first program when I started at WCCO was called
"On the Go." Little did I know how well that would describe my career at the station.

The two of us work hard on these trips, especially Ramona, who does pre-trip research into the countries we're
visiting to make the trip more meaningful to everyone. The
final night, we give out "awards," in the form of postcards
from the countries we have visited. For example, we once
gave the "Twins Award" to one of our group who was a
devoted Twins fan. His card showed a picture of a pair of
Austrian twin children, in local costume. Throughout the
trip, I would work each day on a poem covering the jour-
ney chronologically, which I read at the end of the trip. It
helps put the trip, the pictures, the slides in sequence. This

would be a typical example, from a Southern Germany-Austria-Switzerland tour that took us to Lucerne, Switzerland:

"Lucerne . . . Breakfast, musli . . . shopping, mostly,
Pilatus in the haze, so ghostly.
Brienz, wood carvings and houses old.
Back to the Carlton for showers cold.
Then, a night of fondue-dipping, white wine flowing,
Cross-bows, yodeling, Alp-horns blowing.
On to Strasbourg—parlez-vous Francais?
Deutschmarks, not dollars, when you pay."

A couple of explanatory notes on the above: Pilatus is a mountain near Lucerne, Brienz is a nearby town. The hot water didn't work at the Carlton Hotel, and Strasbourg, in France but just across the border from Germany, accepted German money but not American.

Any extra effort Ramona and I put forward is well-rewarded by the companionship of the friendly people, almost entirely WCCO listeners, who make up these groups. Often, they're repeaters. In our most recent trip, to Eastern Europe, 26 of the 40 tour members were making their second, third, or fourth trip with us.

It's this special bond between all the people connected with WCCO Radio that has earned it the title of "Good Neighbor."

I could feel this relationship with WCCO long before I went to work for them. I, too, was a regular listener as I grew up. This was during the time that Cedric Adams ruled the airwaves on WCCO. He died the year before I started at the station, but his influence was still felt. I really think he had the greatest impact on the WCCO audience of anyone who ever worked for the station. Cedric had an incredible following, both on WCCO and also in his newspaper column in the *Minneapolis Star*. People reacted to

More than anyone else, Cedric Adams epitomized the
"Good Neighbor" image of WCCO. *WCCO Radio*

Jergen Nash with his "mangy, flea-bitten" cat.
That cat sometimes got as much mail from listeners
as Jergen did. *WCCO Radio*

Among other things, Charlie Boone and Roger Erickson were known for their "Worst Jokes of the Week." In the 1970s they put out their own jokebook. *WCCO Radio*

Believe it or not, this picture shows Morgan Mundane, Ma Linger, Backlash LaRue, and Steve Cannon. *WCCO Radio*

Anita Bryant was a guest during the State Fair one year.

In the early 1990s, WCCO built a new studio with so many bells and whistles that we call it our "Star Wars Studio." While it was under construction, though, it became Ray's Place for a day. No actual beverages were dispensed. The "foaming beer" was soapy water. *WCCO Radio*

Hong Kong is a great place to visit. Ramona and I were there in 1988.

We visited Stalheim, Norway, in 1979.

China in 1987.

him. They wanted him in their home. To his listeners and readers, he was known only as "Cedric," not "Mr. Adams" or even "Cedric Adams," just "Cedric." Beyond any other factor, we became the "Good Neighbor" station because of Cedric. He *was* WCCO.

Another legend from that period was sportscaster Halsey Hall. As it was with Cedric, people were on a first-name basis with Halsey. For many years, Halsey and Cedric shared a half-hour news block (sandwiched around a five-minute news commentary by E. W. Ziebarth) each night at 10:00. This news block with Halsey and Cedric was so popular that pilots reported seeing the lights in homes darken throughout WCCO's broadcast area each night at 10:30 when the news ended.

Like Cedric, Halsey went back many years in Twin Cities sports, both covering them for the newspaper and doing play-by-play on the radio in addition to his regular sports show. I had gotten to know Halsey personally when I started broadcasting Gopher football on KUOM. Halsey had been announcing Minnesota football on other stations since Bernie Bierman's first national championship team in 1934. Even though I was from a rival station, Halsey was very helpful and accommodating.

When I started at WCCO, Halsey was a member of the Minnesota Twins' broadcast team with Ray Scott and Herb Carneal. A few years later I had the chance to work with Halsey—and Herb—when I joined the broadcast crew.

Another WCCO personality I "grew up" with was Clellan Card, a very funny man known for his Swedish dialect and light-hearted banter. On his morning program he invited listeners to join him for coffee and doughnut dunking, but as he always said, "No fair dunking above the second knuckle." Every Christmas for 30 years, he actually donned a nightgown and nightcap to read "The Night Before Christmas." He was probably best remembered, though, for the way he wrapped up his program each morning. In his best Swedish accent, he'd read his "birdie" poem. The first three lines were always the same, but the final line was a pun or play on words of some type. One example was, "Birdie with the yellow bill, Hopped upon my window sill, Cocked a shining eye and said, What did you do with the light . . . socket?" Of all the puns he came up with to finish that poem, one of my favorites came in the early 1960s when Vic Power played first base for the Twins: "What's the secret of hitting, Vic . . . Power?"

By the time I started at WCCO Radio, Clellan had switched to WCCO-TV where he played the role of Axel in a children's show called "Axel and the Tree House." I never met Clellan in person, but he used to call me every once in while when I was doing "On the Go." He'd call when I had a record on, and we'd talk off the air for a few minutes. For awhile, he called every couple of weeks. When Clellan died of cancer early in 1966, I truly mourned him as a friend, even though we had never met face-to-face.

Listeners of our station, however, know that dialects on WCCO didn't disappear when Clellan Card left. They have been very ably continued by Roger Erickson and his long-time partner, Charlie Boone. Rog and I had worked together at KUOM playing on-the-air characters created by Betty Girling. These characters have re-emerged, often with Swedish accents, in different forms at WCCO in the skits that have become such a staple of the "Boone & Erickson" show.

Roger was always the first one in for his "Top of the Morning" program that preceded the "Boone & Erickson" show. For many years, he was joined by Maynard Speece, the station's farm director and quite a character himself. In those pre-dawn hours, those two could get away with some material that was a bit more ribald than they would dare try later in the day. Farmers and city folk alike, listening that early, loved the two.

Like Roger, Charlie Boone can do a variety of voices. For years he has provided the voices for the lawyers and clients on both sides in the "Point of Law" show, which airs every weekday afternoon at 5:30. He also has a special ability to make people he's interviewing feel a little better about themselves than they did before the conversation began.

I've often had the chance to fill in for Charlie or Roger when one or the other was on vacation. It was great fun to become half of the "Boone & Erickson" show. When I teamed up with Roger, it was like living KUOM days all over again.

I also joined Roger sometimes in singing the "Good Morning" song around 6:00. They were singing that song when I started at WCCO and they're still singing it each morning. The song is from the musical, "Singin' in the Rain." There's a segment we play in which there are four women saying "good morning." It's followed by an instrumental version of the song, and that's when Roger, Chuck Lilligren, Bill Farmer, and I would chime in: "Good morning, good morning, it's grand to be on hand, good morning, good morning to you." Sometimes we'd even have listeners call in to sing with us. The most important thing was, we weren't supposed to sing it well. Worse was better. On our WCCO tours, I start each day on the bus by leading the group in the "Good Morning" song. If we are in another country, we do part of it in that language. For example, in Germany we sing, "Guten morgen, Guten morgen . . . "

Doing the song back home on WCCO, we'd always introduce the song by saying good morning to cities and towns in Minnesota. When I had the chance to do it, I'd come up with a theme. The theme one morning might be trees. So we'd say, "Good morning, Elmwood! Good morning, Oakdale! Good morning, Pine City! Good morning, Maple Lake!" and then into the song.

Charlie and Roger are always a delight to be with, on and off the air. Maybe that's the secret to their success and longevity. The "Boone & Erickson" combination has stood the test of time, I think, not just because both men are so talented, but because both are just plain good people.

Two other people who were a big part of the WCCO broadcast day for many years were Howard Viken and Joyce Lamont, who now are at KLBB Radio in the Twin Cities along with WCCO alumni Chuck Lilligren and Franklin Hobbs.

Howard had a show at 5:00 A.M. when he started at WCCO in 1950. Later he gave way to Roger Erickson on the early hours, and settled into a time between Roger's early-morning slot and the "Boone & Erickson" show. Howard was so easy to listen to and so easy to get along with. My lasting memory of Howard is hearing him, time after time, read an upcoming commercial out loud, *off* the air, to make sure he would read it right *on* the air.

Joyce was our community and special events director who would pop in and out of the various shows during the day, announcing upcoming events in the Twin Cities. She also had shows about food and recipes. She is a wonderful lady. Whenever Joyce enters a room, the wilted flowers spring back to life.

For a time, we even had "Dear Abby" in our studios on a regular basis. Abigail Van Buren read letters and offered advice over the radio. Actually, this was a CBS program, but since she lived in Minneapolis at the time, the program originated from WCCO.

Sid Hartman is another person who was there when I

started (and still is). In addition to his sports column in the *Minneapolis Star Tribune*, Sid does a number of sports broadcasts on WCCO every morning and afternoon as well as his Sunday morning "Sports Huddle" with Dave Mona.

No one works harder than Sid. No one.

Steve Cannon joined WCCO in 1971, coming from cross-town rival KSTP. With Steve came his theme song, played by the Eveleth City Band, and his on-air alter egos, Ma Linger, Backlash LaRue, and the great prognosticator, Morgan Mundane. I've often been asked if those characters are real. I say they are as close to real as is humanly possible. They're definitely real to Cannon.

Steve loves to tell of the time a football booster club called him and asked if Morgan Mundane could appear at their luncheon and talk football. Steve realized they didn't know that Morgan was a creature of his own voice, but he played along anyway, telling them that Morgan was too busy and wouldn't be able to do it. They then asked Cannon if he would speak to the group instead. Steve pretended his feelings were hurt and said, "You only want me because you can't get Morgan? Forget it!"

Eric Eskola and Ruth Koscielak also come to mind. Eric is the consummate news man, but, beyond that, an exhilarating broadcast partner for the high-school basketball and hockey championships we shared. In late 1992, the station decided not to carry the state high-school Class AA football championship. Had it aired, Eric and I would have been the broadcasters. We spent the next month, embellishing (off the air) "the greatest broadcast that never was."

Ruth has a great ability to make the interviewee feel "wanted" and "listened to." She also does the best elephant trumpet I've ever heard.

Finally, I have to mention Jergen Nash, who was special to me.

I went back with Jergen, as I do with Roger Erickson, all the way to our days at KUOM. Jergen was doing the newscasts at the time I joined him at WCCO. He also hosted a number of shows featuring semi-classical music. His death in March of 1993 brought out any number of Jergen stories. I remember him as always delighting in saying outlandish things, always in the hope of being *thought* of as outlandish. "Well, I think I'll go shoot the program director and then head for home," was a typical Jergen statement. When he talked of his cat, "mangy" and "flea-bitten" were just a couple of the derogatory terms he used, but everybody knew that he loved that cat. Typical of what you'd expect from our listeners, his cat got more than its share of mail.

Jergen worked regularly until 1980. Thereafter, he did a five-minute vignette once a week. Often he taped the programs while traveling in England or Scotland, where his wife, Mary, was from. He'd tell what was happening in their travels. If he was at home, he would talk about whatever happened to strike his fancy back here. "The Passing Parade" was his program and he did it right up to the very end. He will certainly be missed.

My duties have changed at WCCO over the years. For a while, I was doing "Tower Weather" every afternoon at 4:55 P.M. (I mentioned this earlier in relating the bomb threat I experienced at Met Stadium in 1970.) In the late 1960s, I went through the same thing at the Foshay Tower, from where we actually broadcast the weather show. It was a little nerve-wracking to get a report of a bomb when you were on the 30th floor of a 31-story building. My main hope at the time was that they wouldn't evacuate the Foshay Tower until after I had completed the weather. A couple of minutes before I went on the air, however, we got the order to clear out. Fortunately, the elevators were still running through all of this. I would have hated to walk 30 flights of stairs, even if the direction was down.

I now do 12 newscasts/sportscasts from 10:30 to 5:15 each weekday. The newsroom is a *working* room, but it's also a place for wonderfully irreverent humor. Editors Steve Murphy and Rich Holter and reporters Dick Chapman, Bruce Hagevik, Telly Mamayek, and Brooke Aulvin take the news seriously, but we do not take each other seriously.

I was a news reader from the time I began at WCCO in late July of 1963. Even though sports was a minor part of my job those first months, Paul Giel and I broadcast the High School Football Game of the Week every Friday evening that fall. I also filled in for Ray Scott on the Gophers' final football game of 1963 after it was postponed because of the Kennedy assassination. By the following season, I was doing the Gopher games full-time.

I also had the chance to continue with Gopher basketball broadcasting. Dick Enroth, who had done the games, was running for political office and had to give up his announcing duties.

Recently, WCCO Radio was purchased by its network "parent," CBS. While being owned by CBS contains many advantages, it's difficult to keep intact the family feeling we've had during the time that WCCO was independently owned.

I think back to something that happened in March of 1990, when I was in Richmond, Virginia, with the Gophers for the opening rounds of the NCAA Basketball Tournament. The Gophers won on Friday and had another game on Sunday. In between, I received a call from a CBS television producer, asking if I would record an interview with Brent Musberger. It would be used before the telecast of the Gophers' next game. They wanted to record the interview at the arena on Sunday at noon. I told them I would be happy to do the interview, and that I would be going to 11:00 Mass but would be able to get to the arena by ten minutes after twelve. The producer said, "Nope, it's 12:00 or nothing." I told him it would have to be nothing.

On my own pre-game broadcast for the Gopher game, I told the story of what had happened, ending with the comment, "I realize this is contrary to some opinions, but network television is not God."

Now I'm employed by CBS. Although I'm in radio and the 1990 incident was television, I do worry that WCCO Radio may lose the "Good Neighbor" image and individuality that have made it unique in this market and nationally.

For more than 30 years, this has been my second family—both the people I work with and those I broadcast to. I pray we do not forget how we got where we are.

Genuine Thrills

I felt numb as I stepped up to the microphone.

I was in the middle of my 400th broadcast of a Minnesota Gopher football game. I'd always felt a bit nervous before going on the air for each of those games, but this time the feeling was different. So was the situation.

This time my words were not going over the broadcast airwaves, but to the more than 60,000 football fans gathered in the Hubert H. Humphrey Metrodome for the Minnesota Gophers' final game of the 1990 season.

This was a halftime ceremony to mark both my 400th game and the completion of my 40th year announcing Golden Gopher football.

The event had been preceded by a lot of publicity, almost an embarrassing amount. The *Minneapolis Star Tribune* had done a lengthy profile the previous Sunday, chronicling my years covering a variety of sports in Minnesota.

I remember the one feeling I had all that week – it's a feeling I don't usually permit myself – I wanted the Gophers to win. I tried to wipe that out. It's okay to hope they'll play their best, and you'd like to have them win, but you don't make it an overriding thing. In this case it was, and I couldn't get rid of that feeling.

Added to the anticipation of being honored at halftime was the fact that the game was against the Gophers' arch-rival, the Iowa Hawkeyes, who were hoping to win the Big

Ten title and go to the Rose Bowl in Pasadena, California. The Gophers, on the other hand, were 5-5 coming into the game and were just hoping to finish the season with a winning record. The Hawkeyes were favored to win by 14 points.

The Gophers came out battling. It was an exciting first half and Minnesota went into the locker room with a 21-10 lead. It looked encouraging, but an 11-point lead over a team like Iowa was hardly insurmountable.

By this time, I had more to worry about than the score of the game.

There was only 15 minutes between halves, and, in that time, I'd have to hustle down to the field, participate in the ceremony, and then get back to the broadcast booth in time for the start of the second half. My son Jim, who also does my statistics, came with me. Along the way we were met by Jim's wife, Rose, my wife, Ramona, and our daughter, Sue. (Our other son, Tom, and his wife, Ann, who live in Colorado Springs, were unable to attend.) They stood at the sideline as I walked out onto the field.

Stadium announcer Dick Jonckowski began reading from a prepared text: "Ladies and gentlemen, today we're celebrating a special tradition in Gopher athletics. Forty years ago this fall, Ray Christensen began radio play-by-play broadcasts of Gopher football on the University radio station KUOM . . . "

The others involved in the ceremony—Nils Hasselmo, the president of the University of Minnesota, men's athletic director Rick Bay, and Bud Ericksen, president of the M Club, the society for those who had earned athletic letters at the University—each made a presentation.

I received several gifts, but the most special one was the letterman's jacket Bud Ericksen gave me, which made me an honorary member of the M club. It stands out because, although I am not an athlete myself, I've always admired the athletes at the University, and the M jacket is a symbol of athletic excellence. Even though I earned my M Club membership in an honorary capacity, it's still a thrill. I wear that jacket. It's a nice heavy one, well-suited for Minnesota weather.

Finally, it was my turn to speak. Most of all, I wanted to acknowledge the fans who had listened to those broadcasts through the years and made all this possible. I remembered that many of those in attendance this day were Hawkeye supporters, who had come up from Iowa.

As I spoke of enjoying watching 40 years of Gopher football teams, I made a point of mentioning that I also enjoyed watching 40 years of Iowa teams. My final comment, though, was, "With apologies to Iowa fans, Go Gophers!"

As I spoke those words, I shook my fists in the air, which is about as demonstrative as I ever get, then headed back upstairs for the second half.

It was a very nice ceremony, and the Gophers made it a perfect day by beating the Hawkeyes (who still earned a trip to Pasadena as Michigan defeated Ohio State to knock the Buckeyes out of a Rose Bowl berth).

My comments in that halftime ceremony may well summarize my approach to sportscasting. I thought it was only right to acknowledge the Iowa fans by making reference to the 40 years of Iowa football I had seen. It's the same thing when I'm in the broadcast booth. If I ever fail to give credit where credit is due to an opposing player or an opposing team, then I know it'll be time to quit.

At the same time, my wave of the fists and shout of "Go Gophers!" to conclude the ceremony simply pointed out that I am a Gopher fan, that I want the Gophers to do well. My enthusiasm for them often does come through in my broadcasting, and I certainly get more excited about a

Gopher field goal, whether it be in football or basketball, than I do for that of an opponent. I don't try to hide that fact. In a way, I'm fortunate in that I call the games for a particular team, not for a network, where I would have to walk a fine line to avoid showing any partiality.

Actually, I have been in that situation in the past. I broadcast a couple of high school championships in which Minneapolis Roosevelt, my alma mater, participated. I had to be careful not to favor Roosevelt in my commentary, but at the same time not try so hard to be fair that I didn't give Roosevelt its credit. With the Gophers, though, the vast majority of the listeners are pulling for the Gophers, so I feel I darn well better reflect my enthusiasm in what I'm doing. Every year I get a few comments from people who feel I'm too partial toward the Gophers, but I hear from just as many people who say, "Gee, I wish you'd be more partial toward the Gophers." They balance out. I figure as long as that happens, I'm probably doing it about right.

A little over a year after my 400th football game, I reached a milestone in basketball broadcasting. The Gophers' game against Akron on December 11, 1991 was my 1,000th basketball game behind the mike.

Once again, the University held a halftime ceremony to mark the event. To be truthful, I can't say this compared with the festivities at my 400th football game. Maybe it's always a bit less exciting the second time around. I was touched by the presence of Richard Coffey at the basketball ceremony. He was one of the players I admired most in all the years I broadcast those games. Richard had graduated two seasons before, spent a year with the Minnesota Timberwolves, and at this time was playing professionally in Turkey. He was injured, though, and had come home to recuperate. The Gophers, without letting me know, asked him to come to the ceremony and present me with a regulation basketball that read: "Congratulations Ray Christensen. 1,000 Golden Gopher Broadcasts. Minnesota vs. Akron. December 11, 1991. Williams Arena."

It was a genuine thrill.

I have received many awards and recognitions, and I'm grateful for all of them, but there are two others I want to mention specifically:

The Alumni Service Award of the University of Minnesota. I am proud to be a graduate of the university and have tried always to serve it and represent it with respect. The recognition means a great deal.

The title "Honorary Athenan." For the 21 years of the Athena Awards, I have been the master of ceremonies at the awards luncheon in the spring. Each year, I condense onto one small card the many achievements of each of about 50 high-school senior girls who have excelled in athletics and other areas. Then, I read those condensations as each young woman comes to the stage for her award. While my broadcast career has focused on men's sports, I am thrilled by what these women have done, how far they have come, and how much they mean to the future of sports.

The people I've interviewed and the interviewing process itself have also been an important part of my broadcasting career. My basic approach to a guest is one of preparation: know a lot about your guest and about the subject, but, on the air, let that information come from the guest, not from you. The most important thing an interviewer can do is *listen*. I've always felt that if I learn something from an interview, my listeners will learn, too.

Here are some of the more notable people I've had the chance to listen to. I've come away with some lasting impressions from each one.

Sophia Loren. She was very nervous in a radio situation.

She preferred the "clutter" of cameras and all that came with them. We presented her with a red rose, and she was charming and natural. A great smile.

Charlton Heston. He asked me to call him "Chuck." I told him I had seen him too often as a gladiator or a religious leader on a mountain top—he was always "Charlton" to me. The day after our interview, I received a note he had written from his hotel room. It thanked me for the interview and was signed—in quotation marks—"Chuck."

Minnie Pearl. A wonderful lady. A good businesswoman but a completely warm, friendly, next-door-neighbor type.

Mel Torme. He was delighted that I knew he had once played Joe Corntassel on the radio series, "Little Orphan Annie." Torme was in the Twin Cities for a concert with George Shearing, the blind pianist. I had interviewed Shearing several years earlier. What a love for life Shearing has. Sunshine personified.

James Michener. It started out as a non-sports interview with this great novelist, but we wound up talking nothing but sports. I learned far more from him than he did from me.

Alex Haley. I did this interview shortly after "Roots" was published. He was interested in *our* family roots, too.

Buckminster Fuller. His mind, ever scientific, travelled at an incredible speed, usually faster than his ability to form words. A fascinating process.

Jeannette Piccard. From balloonist to Episcopalian priest, this woman conquered every frontier she challenged. A thoughtful, thinking person.

Walter Mondale. Few people maintain so well the balance between "small-town" realism and global perspective. I am proud to have the right to call him "Fritz."

Hubert Humphrey. One of the great thrills of my life

came when I was one of many reporters at a Humphrey media conference. I was with WLOL at the time and hardly a Twin Cities "name." I asked a question, and Hubert began his response by saying, "Well, Ray . . . ." I was so overcome that he knew who I was that his answer completely escaped me.

Ronald Reagan. Before he became president, we did a telephone interview in which we discussed, of all things, re-creating baseball broadcasts using the Western Union ticker service. Some years before, Reagan had re-created Chicago Cubs games while broadcasting on WHO Radio in Des Moines, Iowa. In the interview, he insisted that I call him "Dutch," which was the name he used when he was a sportscaster in Iowa.

Arthur Fiedler. Often described as "crusty," he was just that when he arrived to record an interview. His first words to me were, "Whatever you ask is fine, but let's get it out of the way." I was prepared. The whole thing took ten minutes, and we were through. Before he left, the subject of travel came up. We talked travel. He suggested I give him a tour of the WCCO studios, and we talked more travel. He was warm and friendly and ended up staying for almost an hour.

Leopold Stokowski. This great conductor rarely granted interviews, but when I was at KUOM we made the request anyway. There was no reply. Then, after a morning rehearsal at Northrop Auditorium, Stokowski—alone—decided to walk the two blocks over to our Eddy Hall studios. He announced that he was "here for the interview." I was a young and obviously somewhat-awed announcer, and, I think for that reason, he was a paternal Stokowski rather than an autocratic Stokowski. The interview lasted almost a half-hour, and he stayed for a few minutes afterward just to chat. It was a highlight of an early stage of my broadcasting life.

Dimitri Mitropoulos. He was the conductor of the Minneapolis Symphony Orchestra at the time I knew him. One of the humblest people I have ever met, this man almost always conducted without a score, but when he talked with me, as with anyone, he made me feel as if this was the most interesting conversation of his day.

Theodore Gesell, "Dr. Suess." I have read his words so many times to my children (and continue to read them to my grandchildren) that he is a part of me. I don't know if I conveyed my appreciation strongly enough. I hope I did. There have been many imitators, but only one Dr. Suess.

The interview list goes on and on: a variety of governors, Supreme Court justices, Nobel Prize winners, authors, entertainers, attorneys, but the ones I have listed may capture the flavor of a fascinating segment of my broadcasting career.

Finally, there's "G. T.," which stands for "Great Tiger." She was a 400-pound tiger who wrestled those brave enough to volunteer at sports shows. I did a live interview with her. I have always admired the lithe grace of these big cats, so I enjoyed it. Her attendant, using a chain and choke collar, kept a rein on G. T. Her teeth were real, and she started to chew on the cord of my hand mike. I sweet-talked her off the cord, and then she began licking my shoes. I'm not a very conscientious shoe-polisher, so there couldn't have been any palatable wax. But, for whatever reason, she did a thorough cleaning job on both shoes. I asked G. T. various questions, and her answers were a "purring" sound that at times seemed almost like a bovine "moo." Her attendant had warned me that if she liked me, she might jump up on me. Near the end of the brief interview, she did just that. We were still on the air. Four-

"Go Gophers!" I shout at the conclusion of the ceremony
for my 400th Gopher football game.

I didn't know until I saw this picture that the band had formed a
large "C" behind me during the presentation. *WCCO Radio*

After 35 years of announcing Gopher basketball, I reached the milestone of my 1,000th game.

That's acting athletic director Dan Meinert about to give me the jersey. I felt honored that Richard Coffey, on my left, would share this ceremony.

Roger Erickson (back turned) and I gave Sophia Loren a rose to try to calm her nerves before this interview. It worked. *WCCO Radio*

Mel Torme is one of my favorite performers in addition to being the subject of a memorable interview. *WCCO Radio*

I had the chance to interview Mitch Miller, not on the air but to a live audience during a noon-hour event at the Crystal Court in the IDS. *WCCO Radio*

The interview I remember best may have been with G. T., the tiger. Charlie Boone helps me to keep G. T. calm. *WCCO Radio*

hundred pounds versus 155 pounds is a mismatch, but the attendant held on tight, and it was a matter of affection, not intent to do harm.

I liked G. T., and I'm pleased that she recognized that fact.

Other things that mean a lot:

When a listener and I meet for the first time and the listener says, "You sound just like you do on the radio." I hear it often, and I never tire of it.

The drained feeling I have after an exciting broadcast. It's complete satisfaction. Perhaps "energy well spent" covers it.

When a blind person recognizes my voice after just a very few words. Here is the listener who "listens."

Working with radio technicians through the years. There is a special bond that exists, or at least should exist, between the announcer and the engineer. Often it's unspoken but no less strong.

Conversations in the hallways and offices at WCCO with just about anybody. It's an integral and stimulating part of each day.

Thousands of times, I have concluded a newscast and given a station break so that it all ends when the second hand is straight-up on the clock, at which time the "CBS News" is triggered. It's a very minor challenge, but I still feel rewarded each time we make that "straight-up" connection.

Radio is and always will be very important to me, but I do not bring it home with me. "Home" means "Family," and that supersedes everything else.

My grandson Brian had a card and a hug
for me on Father's Day in 1992.

Family

The longest hallway in our home contains many photos of our family, from grandchildren to ancestors of over 100 years ago. It also contains this framed poem:

> "Our family is like a patchwork quilt
>   with kindness gently sewn.
> Each piece is an original
>   with beauty of its own.
> With threads of warmth and happiness
>   it's tightly stitched together
> To last in love throughout the years.
>   Our family is forever."

This is a difficult chapter to write. I consider our family to be very close, and it's hard to stand off to one side and observe. Ramona and I have three children: Tom, Sue, and Jim. Tom is married to Ann. They have a three-year-old daughter, Emily, and a brand-new summer arrival, Mary Ellen. Emily is learning that her plan to teach the baby to walk as soon as it arrived needs to be modified. Jim is married to Rose, and they have two boys—five-year-old Brian and two-and-a-half-year-old David. Tom lives in Colorado Springs, Colorado. Sue and Jim live in the Twin Cities area.

We are very proud of Tom and Ann, Sue, Jim and Rose. They were good kids, and they're responsible adults. All five understand that life is far too serious to take it too seriously, and when we get together there's always a lot of laughter. Ramona's mother, Margaret, is in her 90s and still very active, especially with her great-grandchildren.

I think Ramona and I have been good parents, but I think we've been lucky, too. Tom, Sue, and Jim have all been active in music. All three took piano lessons (the stress of an important play-by-play broadcast is nothing compared with the stress of listening to your child in a piano recital). Tom plays the string bass, Sue the clarinet, and Jim the tenor saxophone (including five years with the U of M Marching Band). Being involved with music groups has been stimulating to their growth. All three have been willing to take on leadership roles. All three tackle life head-on.

Tom and Jim graduated from the University of Minnesota; Sue is a St. Olaf College grad. Tom went on to get his masters' and doctorate at Cornell University in Ithaca, New York. All three have become quite proficient at handyman chores, from hanging wallpaper to putting up sheet rock to "you-name-it." This inclination and ability come from their mother, who is much better at it than I. I can change a tire and lay sod, but not much beyond that.

Our children have an interest in sports, with Sue and Jim the most keenly involved. Those two are deep into sports, the players, the strategies. Jim may have an edge in college sports, but Sue reigns supreme when the subject is the Minnesota Twins. Jim has kept my individual and team statistics in football and basketball home games for the past 15 years. One of the joys of my life is standing side-by-side with him before a game, singing the national anthem.

Ramona and our children share my love for words and for a good (or bad) pun. Tom is the pun leader. It's hereditary and incurable.

Ramona and I also have had two children who died.

John, our first born, was a premie and lived less than a day. Mary Beth was born after Tom. She lived 13 months with a two-chambered heart. Although she never had the strength of other infants her age, she was sweetness personified. Mary Beth taught us a great deal.

Ramona and I met at KUOM at the University of Minnesota, where we both spent many hours with the Radio Guild, which helped to bring to the air the many dramatic broadcasts of the Minnesota School of the Air (in-school listening, from kindergarten to high school). When Ramona graduated from the University and then went to Rice Lake, Wisconsin, to teach high school speech and English, each weekend found me driving to Rice Lake or Ramona coming home by bus. We were married in November of 1953. Ramona then taught at Elk River High School until our family began.

Especially in our early years, when my sports travels were more a year-round occupation, Ramona had to be both father and mother. I tried to be with the family as much as possible, but hers was the real burden. She carried it extremely well.

Perhaps some random thoughts will explain what our life together—Ramona's and mine—is like:

When we're driving somewhere, we're often silent and perfectly content with just being together.

When I'm on a Gopher trip, I leave a note or two behind and find a note or two in my bag.

Once, shortly before we were married, Ramona called me a "silly goose," a term of endearment. Since then, we have collected geese, mostly porcelain. Not many lately. You can only find shelves for so many geese.

213

We're both still excited when a cardinal comes to our bird feeder.

In our trips, we enjoy equally a white mountain peak or a glistening fjord, or a small detail on an 18th-century building, a child playing by a fountain, or a sunrise, or a sunset.

Unquestionably, we are closer in our lives to the sunset than we are to the sunrise. But the sun sets slowly and beautifully, and we intend to enjoy every minute of it.

H. C. and Me

In June of 1982, the Danish Day committee asked me to speak at the annual get-together in Waubun Park, near Minnehaha Falls in south Minneapolis. I had spoken there just a couple of years before, so this time the committee suggested that I do a reading from Hans Christian Andersen, the famed Danish author.

I decided to add a little to the reading. I was able to rent a costume from the International Institute, including a top hat, cape, black tie, and carpet bag . . . all similar to what H. C. used to wear. I added props, like the rope he always carried in his travels. (If there was a fire when he was above the main floor, he wanted to be ready.)

In the presentation itself, I would begin by playing the part of H. C. Andersen, in Danish dialect, describing "my" childhood and early adult life. Then I would put on my glasses, explaining that Andersen's works were translated into almost every language, and that these were my "American spectacles." This enabled me to read the story or stories in my own "American" voice.

The presentation at Waubun Park went over well and became popular enough that I did it at various Scandinavian functions, mostly Danish, but for some Swedish, Norwegian, and Finnish groups, as well.

The most meaningful took place in Elk Horn, Iowa, on May 23, 1985. The temporary stage was set up about 100 yards from a Lutheran church that had replaced an earlier Lutheran church. In that original church, 100 years and one day earlier, my grandmother—on her 21st birthday—was married. On this occasion, instead of beginning my presentation as Hans Christian Andersen, I began as myself, explaining the emotion I felt and the reason for it. Then, I switched over to H. C.

My second-most meaningful performance came three months later in the Danish community of Askov, Minnesota, where Grandmother had lived and where my mother had grown up. I played H. C. Andersen in the village park, just three houses east of what was once my grandmother's house. When I was a boy, I used to spend two or three weeks of my summer vacation at that house. Grandmother was *Bedstemor* to me, and we always talked Danish, as did a lot of people around Askov in those days.

The front porch is gone, but Grandmother's house is still there—and all the windows remain. My grandmother wanted a lot of windows, and that's how my grandfather had designed and built the house. (For a farmer, he was also a pretty fair architect-contractor.) The hollyhocks on the east side are gone, too, so the house looks different, but the memories are still vivid.

I'm sure the inside has changed: no wood stove where she baked bread and rolls every afternoon (only to see them disappear before supper), no red hand-pump at the kitchen sink any more, and no dumbwaiter with the wooden crank to bring up milk and cream from the cool earthen cellar.

There are still plenty of dirt roads in Askov. I kicked a few stones, as I had done as a boy, walking from the depot over to the park. The depot is a museum now, and a good one, and the dispatcher's telegraph and other equipment

In 1953 Ramona and I were married.

Tom, our oldest son, was born in December, 1956.

Tom and his wife, Ann, with their daughter, Emily. They have since had another daughter, Mary Ellen.

Our daughter, Sue.

Believe it or not, this is our son, Jim. Jim served as Goldy Gopher for women's games, but he also filled in as Goldy for a men's game in 1985.

Jim and his wife, Rose, with their sons, David and Brian.

Ramona and me, on our 35th wedding anniversary, 1988.

We had the whole family together for Christmas in 1991. From left to right are
Sue, Tom, Emily, Ann, Jim, Brian, David, and Rose.

Brian

David

Emily

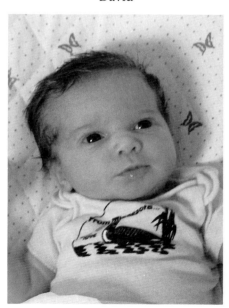

Mary Ellen

are sitting in the bay window, just a few feet from the double train tracks, which are still in use.

When I visited my grandmother, I would go down to the main crossing every evening at 6:00 to watch the "Flyer" from Duluth to the Twin Cities grab the mail bag that was hung from a hook on the downtown side of the tracks. That bag was picked up by a mechanical arm projecting from the train, but the mail bag *for* Askov was thrown out by hand. It was always a game to guess where it would land.

Downtown Askov is different now but not a lot. It's still one block long. Pedersen's Store isn't a variety store anymore. Some of the other buildings have changed character, too. I wonder if everybody still comes into town on Saturday night. I remember it as a night mostly for conversation, although there was a small band that used to play in front of the town hall. The town hall is still there, filled with memorabilia.

The cemetery, just west of town, is well maintained. My grandparents and some of my uncles and aunts are buried there. Almost all the Danish names on the markers are familiar to me, whether I actually knew the people or not.

And the Park. The bandstand is surrounded by grassy slopes that create a natural amphitheater, and that's where I did my portrayal of Hans Christian Andersen. As a boy, I used to go to the park every Wednesday evening to watch Askov play a team from one of the nearby towns—Bruno or Finlayson or Kerrick—in a softball game. That was an "event" and always drew a big crowd. On Sunday afternoon everybody used to gather for the hardball game in the southwest corner of town. There was a small grandstand, but a lot of the fans watched from their cars. They'd sit on top, then lean inside to honk the horn whenever Askov scored a run. That baseball park is gone now.

Many memories of the Danish author are brought to

light in my portrayal of Hans Christian Andersen. As you can tell, he brings out a few of my own—a wedding one hundred years earlier, a return to Askov, and a ball game.

Final Wrap

In the nearly half-a-century I've been involved in radio broadcasting, one of my favorite programs was a series I did on WCCO from the middle of 1980 until just into 1986. It aired at 11:05 every Saturday morning and was made up of whatever I decided to talk about that week.

In closing, here is the script from the last program in that series, the "final wrap," just as I wrote it and read it.

Saturday 11 January 1986
Beginning next Saturday, this program will change its focus, so this is my last time around.

How do you conclude a series? I realized that I wasn't even sure that there's been any pattern to what I've done. These weekly five minutes have, for better or worse, been me.

Sometimes they've been personal . . . if I was locked in the bathroom, and I thought there was humor in the situation, I talked about it. Humor should be shared.

The words of others should be shared, too. Men and women far wiser than me have thought about life and put those thoughts into words. Whether those words were expressed three or four years ago or three or four centuries ago, they are relevant.

I am, by nature, curious, and when I have learned about something new and interesting to me, I have tried to dig a little deeper into the subject and tell you what I learned. Curiosity and the willingness to *do* something about it are part of what makes life stimulating. Getting back to famous thoughts, I have a plaque my father lettered. The words on it, origin unknown, are these: "It's what you learn after you know it all that counts."

Music is an essential part of my life, and, occasionally, I have devoted a program to it. I have often thought it would be the best of all worlds to be a composer—a good one—and to put notes on paper that conductors or soloists would bring to life long after I am gone.

I have an undying respect for the English language, and I hope I make that clear. Sports play-by-play is a big challenge. The cliche grows readily, like a weed, in the stadium and arena.

Ramona and I have been blessed with many opportunities to travel, and I have shared those trips with you— partly because other parts of the world are fascinating in their *differences* and partly because other *peoples* of the world are *not* so different from you and me.

I try to take time to smell the roses. Cardinals and chickadees, sunsets and waterfalls, the first crocus and the turning leaves, an old building and a new book . . . they all deserve our attention.

I have talked of my family—Ramona and our children, Tom, Sue, and Jim. They are very important to me. When Tom published his doctoral thesis this past summer—200 pages representing six years, 12 months a year, of studies and research into the oxidation of metals, ellipsometry, and other wonders of applied physics—he inscribed on the dedication page: "To my parents, who taught me so much more." I cannot put into words how much that means to us.

The family should be where love begins, but love goes

beyond that. In a world in which Love and Hate are in an endless struggle, we must have faith that love will win. There are so many forces of hate, but it is still far easier to love than to hate. Try it. You'll like it.

One final quotation on this last program of these five-and-a-half years . . . Oscar Hammerstein used it as a lead-in to his song, "16 Going on 17," from *The Sound of Music:*

A bell is not a bell 'til it's ringing
A song is not a song 'til it's singing
And love in your heart was not put there to stay
Love is not love 'til you give it away.

This is Ray Christensen.

Index

Index

Index